Now

Anne Townsend [qualified at the Royal] Free Hospital, London and then worked as a missionary doctor in Thailand for sixteen years, with her husband. During that time she also helped produce literature in the Thai language.

Since their return to England Anne has been founding editor of *Family* magazine and is currently Director of *Care Trust* (Christian Action Research Education) in London. She has written for a number of Christian publications and is the author of ten books, several concerned with family life. Her interests include knitting and gardening.

She and her husband John – a surgeon – have three grown-up children and live in Surrey.

ANNE TOWNSEND

Now and For Ever

Collins
FOUNT PAPERBACKS

First published by Fount Paperbacks, London in 1986

Copyright © Anne Townsend 1986

Made and printed in Great Britain by
William Collins Sons & Co. Ltd, Glasgow

To John, my husband,
with love and appreciation
for our first twenty-five
years together

Chapter 1

It's a quarter of a century since I walked, on my father's arm, along the path lined with cow parsley to the tiny church where John and I were married. But John and I are no longer the naïve couple who went down that aisle. We have grown, and much of that growth has come about through the struggles and pains of learning what marriage means today.

Attaining silver-wedding status has made me look long and hard at my marriage to try to learn from it. Those twenty-five years have seen marked changes, not only in John and me but also in the society in which we live, for this has been a time in which attitudes towards marriage have changed more quickly and more dramatically than during any other period of history.

Marriage, as I see it, and as I believe the Bible teaches, is basically about a deep, exclusive, and very special relationship between a man and a woman. Such a relationship is unique in that it is intended to be for life, and is designed for the greatest good not only of the couple concerned, but also for those who are around them, and for the whole of society and national life. There are other components – mutual support, the running of a home, the rearing of children, and the sharing of responsibility for one another's relatives as well as for one's own. But these are secondary to the main function of marriage as God has created it to be. In the words of the Bible: "The Lord God said, 'It is not good for the man to be alone. I will make a helper suitable for him.' . . . Then the Lord God made a woman from the rib he had taken out of the man, and he brought her to the man. The man said, 'This is now bone of my bones and flesh of my flesh; she shall be called

7

"woman", for she was taken out of man'" (Genesis 2:18, 22–25).

But deep and meaningful relationships rarely occur instantaneously – they take years of work, sharing, cultivation and growth through the development of a kind of understanding of one another that can be as painful as it is constructive, as John and I were to find.

What John and I have been through together has marked and changed us both individually and as a couple. I have studied these changes and I am now aware of them as I never was before. I see them as they are and not as I think they ought to be. One of the things that has most shaped our marriage is our particular lifestyle – the fact that we are a couple of doctors, who have worked overseas as missionaries, and who are committed Christians. It is only recently that I have been able to think about particular events in our lives, and see how they have fitted together to make our marriage – for better or worse – what it now is. Coming to terms with my husband's vocation has been one of the main factors that has made me try honestly to face and learn from my own marriage.

"Darling," John began one morning eighteen years ago, when we had been in Thailand as missionary doctors for just three years. He looked at the wall and not at me. "I really need to be a better surgeon."

I couldn't disagree. At that time, John was operating in relatively primitive conditions. It was a miracle that some of his critically ill patients did as well as they did, as he had had minimal surgical training.

There was no alternative – we both knew that as a medical missionary John needed to be the best doctor that he possibly could be. "All right – go and train as a surgeon next leave . . ." I wearily agreed, knowing full well that the price to be paid was not just the expense of courses and exam fees; the price would be our relationship. So, John lived and studied in London, and the three children and I stayed with my parents. I waited and longed for those alternate weekends when my man came home again.

Once John's first set of exams were passed, he embarked on a rigorous series of hospital jobs to qualify him to take his finals. That meant frequent weekends and nights on duty, and evenings studying. I knew that as a good missionary wife I ought to be supporting my husband. But everything in me cried out: "Don't do it! Stay with me and the children. Give us time to be yours. Be with us!"

During those months of John's intensive training, I learned what it was like to be head of a single-parent family. I learned how to live without depending on a husband's help, and how to cope with the hard work of bringing up young children alone. Peace came only in the evening – sitting looking out across Stoke-on-Trent's orange night sky, with the pits belching fumes, kilns gleaming in the flickering neon cinema signs, and railway trucks winding through the valley shipping coal and steel from mines to ports. Even now the night sky over the Potteries spells to me the loneliness of a single parent.

Once gained, that degree was *John*'s pride and not something we had achieved together. I was left feeling I had given up a lot (I had just about lost my husband for two years) and gained nothing. Our relationship had turned into one of lovers who have little to say to each other – it was a long time since each had given adequate time to understand the other.

On our return to Thailand, with John now fully qualified as a surgeon, I chided myself in my more cynical and self-pitying moments: "You fool! Look what's happened now. Your husband's become one of the small surgical team, and that means he'll be around even less than he was before."

These thoughts were followed by weeks of misery and self-pity that were usually terminated by my desperate attempt to be the kind of Christian I thought I ought to be, and by really trying not to mind what was happening to me.

If consecration to Christ involved losing my husband to what seemed to be God's service, then I was determined to try not to thwart his will. I believed that if I was going to be a good missionary and a faithful servant of Jesus Christ, then I should not put pressure on John to keep him from the operating-room, his administrative office, or from sharing the Gospel with non-Christians whenever he thought he should. Yet at the same time I often longed for him to say he wanted to come home and spend time talking and sharing with me – understanding me and letting me understand him. It seemed that he was caught up in a work that was greater than the two of us, and in something that I couldn't ask him to wriggle out of.

There were times when I needed to share with John, but the operating-room took priority over everything else. There were times when my children left for boarding school and I needed a husband's hands to hold and comfort me, but those hands always seemed to be saving the lives of other people. As a doctor myself I understood the importance of John's work, and I began to feel that perhaps there was something wrong with my need to be married to a man who would understand me and who would want the same in return. As a missionary I (wrongly) began to believe that my ideals for marriage were an impossible dream. My marriage could not be what I expected, because the man to whom I was married was also wedded to surgery and evangelistic work.

A pattern was set, so that we did well if we spent our wedding anniversary evening on our own together at home (there was nowhere to go out to where we lived in up-country Thailand), and even then a call to an emergency in the operating-room could take John away on that special evening once a year. Children need parents – and we firmly believed that boys need dads. But when Dad is a surgeon and the administrator of an isolated mission hospital, children have to grab him and play with him when they can. We did learn as a family to seize every second John was in the house and to use it, turning it into time for the children. They and he romped, played, read stories and laughed their heads off at funny records.

Perhaps our marriage would have gone on like that for the rest of our lives, but six years ago God's call to John came clearly, simply and definitely.

John had finished the tricky part of an operation and was quietly and patiently putting in rows of delicate stitches to hold different layers of intestines and abdomen together. As he worked peacefully and unhurriedly, with a Bach concerto playing in the background, a voice seemed to speak to him from the far corner of the room. He looked across the bright arc of the theatre lights – no one other than theatre staff was there.

The voice was compelling and authoritative. "Your work in Thailand is now over. I want you back in England making a home for your family. I want you to be a father to your children . . ." And with the knowledge given only to those who have heard God's voice speak to them before, John was certain that this was God's clear call to him. I couldn't even share this experience. My lack of belief when he came home showed itself in shrugged shoulders, and the words: "I'll believe it when it happens!" But happen it did. Within a few months we were settled in England.

When John and I returned to England from Thailand I was so confused at all that was involved in building a totally new life for myself and my family, that it was some months before I began to take a good look at what was happening around me. To my intense surprise, disappointment and disillusionment, I discovered the existence of other Christian marriages in a similar state to John's and mine. The couples concerned were usually unaware of the deterioration in their relationship, or sometimes they were fatalistic, believing there was no hope of change and no escape route – so they acquiesced and left things as they were.

11

I was disappointed, because I had hoped to find out from others how I could be part of a fulfilling, satisfying, joyful Christian marriage in today's secularized and fast-changing society. Some couples to whom I talked had marriages which seemed really "good"; somehow they were the ones to whom I found it hardest to pose the deeply searching questions whose answers might have helped me. Instead, I began to chat to scores of people whose marriages had ended in separation and divorce, as increasingly I was invited to talk to Christian single parents.

This meant that I was not learning *from* other people's mistakes; I was learning their mistakes for myself! I heard from many who had problems identical to mine and I could see how things had gone wrong, but this was not balanced by talking to Christian couples who had somehow got things right and were still together, with happy, well-adjusted and growing marriages. But positive or negative, the end result was the same. I was being forced to look, to assess and to learn about what was happening not only to my own marriage, to marriage generally in Britain, but also to the marriages of some deeply committed Christians.

Even as I looked around me, in a hidden recess of my heart, shared with no one, lurked the longing that not only would John now give his children the opportunity of having a father, but that he would also be able to give his wife a real husband after so many years. I didn't articulate these longings – it seemed selfish for me as a Christian to request some of the time my husband could give to Christian work, when he wasn't with the children. So, I told no one that my dream on our return to England had been that John and I would be able to develop the deep relationship I was sure that God intended us to have.

John's immediate work on return from Thailand was a job with a Christian overseas relief agency which suited his gifts and experience remarkably well. All our married lives we had worked together (apart from John's surgery degree) and even though we had little time to talk, we had shared daily experiences and knew one another's work pressures and problems. I found it difficult to realize that John's new work would involve him being back in Thailand for two weeks every month for six months – the agonizing plight of Cambodian refugees and the Vietnamese boat people made this necessary. This particular assignment was planned around our children's half-terms and exeats from boarding school. I found myself now alone in English suburbia, learning to be a housewife for the first time, and away from Thai and missionary friends. All the kindness from new friends in our new church did not take away my sense of isolation.

I waited some months, hoping that perhaps I might work with John, but no vacancy came up. And, like most missionaries who return home in their mid-forties with teenagers to support, we had no option but for me to work. Having done our sums we realized that a large proportion of John's income would have to go on a mortgage and that my earnings were vital as we set up home in England.

So for the first time in our marriage our work paths diverged. John's job took him overseas for a quarter of the year (the part of his work he loved the best). I found totally unexpected work editing a Christian magazine full-time, and I was increasingly in demand as a speaker at conferences. It was satisfying and demanding for the first time in twenty years of marriage to be a career woman standing on my own feet, and to be carving out a new role in mid-life in a field about which I knew little.

My job satisfaction in some ways compensated for any shallowness in our marriage relationship. If John was abroad, if he was out at a committee meeting in the evening, if he was preoccupied with planning his next overseas trip or in the recovery phase from his last trip, then I didn't mind too much. I found I was no longer dependent on John alone for emotional satisfaction, nor was he the only centre to my life. My comings and goings no longer had to revolve around him. If he wanted to be home late then I could always leave his meal in the microwave and get on and do my own thing – I had plenty with which to occupy myself. But deep within myself I hated the growing distance between the two of us, made worse by those overseas trips.

When John returned, I didn't particularly want to hear what he had been doing. I'd cover my refusal to see the boxes of slides with words like: "They're all the same . . ." But the real reason was that irrationally and illogically I felt semi-betrayed and semi-deserted by a husband who disappeared and lived a quarter of his life totally apart from me. There seemed no way that I could enter into and share in what to him was the most precious part of his job. If he was going to tell me anything about those trips, then what I really wanted to hear was the secret parts, the joys and pains of his heart which he could share with no one else.

Early in the life of *Family* magazine we ran a survey among the readers to try to find out about their marriages. We asked about stress points, and found to our surprise and dismay that a major cause of stress affecting both husbands and wives was the pressure of *church* commitments. In a paradoxical way, that made me feel slightly better. It was a relief to discover that I was not the only one who had faced up to divided loyalties between husband and "things that were being done for God". The pressures I had experienced as a missionary wife and mother were parallel to those being faced by Christian wives and mothers of men who were deeply committed to church work.

Typically male, John shared with me geographical facts and statistics. Typically female, I wanted to know about people, and above all about my own man and how that trip had affected him. But I could not find the key to unlock the secret world in which he lived when he was away from me. It reached the point when one evening when John was abroad,

I asked myself: "Isn't it time to give up trying to get closer to one another?"

The years were rushing by at such speed that the panacea in the past, when we faced marriage ups and downs, of "Never mind, there will be time to work it out later", no longer applied – within a year or so we were supposed to celebrate our silver-wedding anniversary. I did not want to "celebrate" by burying a dead relationship, and accepting as a death certificate a set of divorce papers, as others had. But I had to face the fact that I did not really see how my marriage could continue as it was.

Like many other women at my age and stage of marriage I was beginning to be tired with trying. I was hurt with sharing and then feeling misunderstood. I knew I had to find the courage to face up to what was happening in my own marriage, and to work, with my husband, to try to put things right. We became determined to get our marriage heading in the right direction by our silver-wedding anniversary – which didn't leave us very long to sort things out.

To begin to understand and be understood, when the habit of years has achieved the opposite, is no easy task. A huge bowl of roses in the hearth of our sitting-room was a symbol of real understanding, and the price that must be paid for it. The delicate pinks, glowing apricots, vibrant reds and transparent yellows of roses in blossom were lifted high in their glory and beauty by the very stems that I had pruned severely the previous winter.

For John and me to attain a marriage that paralleled those roses in their perfection, we had to be subjected to pain – the pain of pruning, and the pain of daily living out the price that understanding another person exacts. I believed the price was worth paying, for I knew that the value of our restored marriage relationship could never be assessed.

Chapter 2

Twenty-five years ago marriage breakdown between committed Christians was virtually unknown. Today, reflecting the trend in society generally, it is growing steadily. As I realized this, I felt sad and shocked. Various reports confirmed the grim statistics. Apparently around 25 per cent of couples separate before their fifth wedding anniversary; and there is another divorce peak after twenty years or so of marriage, as the children leave home. The later divorces are harder to prevent.

I had assumed that what was happening to John and me was unusual, and that the effort we had to make to turn our marriage into a stable relationship was the result of the stresses and strains peculiar to the life we had led as missionaries. As I came to understand more about marriage in the 1980s I could see that our experience was not unique or peculiar.

John and I came into the category of "twenty years or more", but by God's grace we were determined to prevent things from getting worse, and to work at improving them. I knew that as a Christian I should not give in and fall prey to discouragement — for the God I serve is a God who takes seemingly hopeless situations and lost causes and redeems them when they are handed over to him. There is no need for me — or for any other committed Christian — to give up on marriage, for within us we have the God-given potential for radical transformation.

However, the massive changes in marriage in the past twenty years cannot be dismissed. These changes have in some way or another affected nearly all marriages, both among committed Christians and among others. Robert

Runcie, Archbishop of Canterbury, stated: "One of the reasons why failure in marriage is a particular problem today is its length. Two hundred years ago the average marriage would have lasted fifteen years, now it's more like fifty. It's a lot to ask young people to be faithful for that length of time, especially when by 'faithful' we mean not just docile, well behaved, but romantic and companionable."[1]

Facts and figures about marriage in its current fragile and fragmented state make for sorry reading. Divorce is an increasing trend (1981 – 146,000; 1976 – 127,000; 1971 – 25,000). There have also been substantial increases in the proportion of divorces which occur early in marriage. In 1981 one in four divorces took place before five years of marriage. It is now reckoned that overall, after thirty years of marriage, one in three can be expected to end in divorce. If present trends continue, nearly three in five marriages in which the husband marries as a teenager would end in divorce before the tenth anniversary. For teenage brides, one marriage in two could be expected to end in divorce by the thirtieth anniversary. Statistics like those make me heavy hearted, especially as divorce followed by remarriage is not notably successful. Lessons have rarely been learned well enough to help the second time round.

Meanwhile, more and more young children are caught in the crossfire of mismanaged adult relationships, and the emotional liability of unstable family life in childhood often affects them as adults. Only three in ten divorces do not include children. In 1981, the parents of 159,000 children under sixteen were divorced. If these trends continue, one in five children will experience their parents' divorce before they reach the age of sixteen.

Each broken marriage can trace its roots back to many different causes. These same causes are often pressure points in those marriages that do survive, and can prove to be growth points when they are worked through and resolved.

Although many of the changes we have faced have been

harmful, there have also been advantages. Thirty years ago Christian teenagers were taught little about contraception and how to handle their sexuality. The permissive sixties had yet to come. For me, thirty years ago, such knowledge was hard to come by. A furtive trip into a large London bookshop, and a detailed examination of *Gray's Anatomy* – one of my set books as a medical student – did not save me from the embarrassment in one physiology lecture of asking what to me seemed a simple, sensible question but which the lecturer and the rest of the class found hilariously funny. Between his choking laughs he managed to turn my cheeks puce by stating: "Little girls like you who don't know all the facts of life should go home and ask their mummies instead of training as doctors . . ."

I didn't go home and ask "mummy" – I was too ashamed by public humiliation at my ignorance. Instead, I slunk around sleazy Soho shops learning an aspect of life which I believe God never intended to be the lot of mankind – the degradation, the sordid trade made out of God's pure gift of sex, the exploitation of women as objects with bodies for sale. The whole thing was sick, and so different from the pure, beautiful and spiritually enriching idea of sexuality which I had learned from my parents and from the Bible. I had seen some of the results of man's sinful independence of God – one of man's many ways of taking God's good gifts and ruining them for selfish gratification. I was sad for those involved but was personally untouched, for my own courtship was simple, pure and lovely.

Like most of my friends, I was a virgin when I married. Our Christian faith made us determined not to consummate our love before marriage. We therefore made sure that we were never in a situation where temptation might lead us to act in ways in which, in cold blood, we did not want to act. Like any normal woman I wanted to be kissed and cuddled –

but we set our personal limits of "so far and no further". We knew when we had to stop as a couple, and respected one another enough to remain within mutually agreed boundaries.

Talking to some modern young women who are now the age I was when I married, I am convinced that we gained rather than lost by waiting until our wedding night to consummate our love for one another. The myth that says that you don't know whether you'll "fit" one another or not unless you try beforehand, is no more than a myth and has no medical basis. Few couples achieve fully satisfactory sexual relations from an emotional point of view outside the security of a loving and committed relationship.

"What have you gained", I asked a younger friend, "by sleeping with those boys?" She was rightly defensive as my words were ill chosen and tactless. She replied: "Well at least I've had many experiences of love – you haven't."

Later, on my own, I wept for her: "Poor kid . . . you've let men use you as an object, and you think that is love. You say that 'there's sex for love and sex for kicks' – but you don't really know what love is. Love isn't sleeping with a man – or another woman for that matter. Love is giving yourself totally to another person with every part of your being, so that its natural expression is the mutual self-giving of sexual intercourse." How could I explain to her that God has given sexual intercourse as a symbol of the unity between a man and a woman who are fully committed to one another. It is not something to be sold, abused or traded.

The difference between that seventeen-year-old's attitudes and mine as a bride, twenty-five years ago, sums up one of the massive differences between many marriages today and the concept of marriage John and I had when we were wed one May heat wave, with the scent of freshly scythed hay drifting across the fields. The sexual revolution of the sixties and seventies has been and almost gone in the years in which we have been married. It has left its mark on us and it has altered the way generations younger than we are look at life.

In the last twenty years, along with the permissive society and new popular ethic that says "You can do anything that feels good as long as no one gets hurt", have come two significant changes in the law. The 1967 Abortion Act has now made the mother's womb a dangerous place for a tiny baby. Since the inception of that law, 2.5 million babies have been legally killed by abortion. Yet, when I was first married and the laws were strict, it was relatively rare for an unborn baby to be killed by "back street abortion" – most were allowed life and were adopted. Legal abortion is now permitted for reasons that some regard as little more than "killing for convenience". The other major changes in family law have been the 1967 Divorce Law and the 1984 Matrimonial Proceedings Act.

The advent of the contraceptive pill and free family-planning services have also considerably changed the status of both married and unmarried women. You cannot help but be aware of contraception. It is assumed in the chemist's that you want sheaths – multicolour, with titillating names – available on the counter; clinics are listed and the names displayed prominently; there is the open media debate about whether girls under sixteen can be put on the pill without parental consent – girls who are under the legal age for consent to sexual intercourse. If a girl today grows up not assuming that the average normal teenager of the 1980s automatically (at some stage or other) goes on the pill "just in case", then she is likely to be the exception. Her generation has received teaching from blatant and subtle messages in teen magazines and papers, many teen-counselling centres, teaching in some schools, and television and radio "agony aunties". They create the impression that "It's okay to sleep around as long as you don't get pregnant." No one warns girls of the possible risk of cervical cancer, AIDS, sexually transmitted diseases, pelvic infection leading to infertility as an adult, and emotional problems in relationships later on.

This availability of the pill has affected the unmarried but it has also affected the married. Sexual intercourse outside marriage can now take place without the deterrent of a possible pregnancy. My generation of wives is more likely to risk an affair outside marriage than they would have been before the pill was available. The post-coital or "morning after" pill has removed another hurdle which in the past stopped some from having casual sex with someone they barely knew for what can be described in terms of "lust" rather than "love".

But for me, as for millions of others, the pill has provided the wonderful and serious responsibility of choosing when to have our children, and of spacing and limiting our family. It has also given us the option of continuing our careers outside the home if we want to, with the assurance that an unexpected pregnancy is unlikely to interrupt a career at a crucial stage. Many Christians have accepted this new gift of freedom without question, but a few ask: "Shouldn't we leave it to God to give us children when he wants us to have them?" So the contraceptive pill has been a major cause of stress in some marriages, and of increased harmony in others.

At the same time, the feminist movement has forced many women to examine and think through their attitude to husband and family. These changes in society have not bypassed the average Christian married couple – but unfortunately few have had the incentive to study secular society and how the underlying assumptions of that society have affected them. Therefore, many Christian couples find themselves wondering, too late, how to alter their situation. Their attitudes to life have changed, and they did not realize what was happening until they looked at who they were when they first married, and compared this with the people who they are now.

The last twenty-five years have also seen a phenomenal increase in the number of women working outside the home. Reasons for this are varied. For some fortunate women – and I include myself among them – a career can complement the husband's work, and can be arranged around the life of husband and children. It can provide a fulfilment which will enrich the home. And we must not forget the particular contribution which women can make to society in their work. But a wife's work can affect – or reflect – the marriage relationship.

I shall never forget the defeat in the eyes of the Liverpool working man who told me: "I was made redundant at forty. The wife brings in the money now. If I want any cash I have to ask her for it. It makes me feel as if I'm living on the earnings of a prostitute. Where I come from men don't live off their wives . . . I'm that ashamed . . . and our marriage is all but finished."

Some of today's wives are working for other reasons. Mary told me: "I'll continue my job after we marry, although we don't need the money. That job's my security in case my marriage doesn't work out. If we split I could go on working without having lost my job, or the promotions I need, just by being married. It's my safety net – and you never know these days, do you, with one in three marriages ending in divorce . . ."

Mary's attitude was wrong. As Christians she and Patrick should have entered marriage firmly convinced that God's plan was for them to be married for life. As Christians they should not have needed to build in safeguards necessary for those who see marriage as impermanent and disposable. Patrick and Mary's marriage vows to one another, in God's presence, ought to have included a firm mutual commitment to make their relationship work.

That couple had never looked at marriage as I did. They had absorbed attitudes from the society in which we live. They noticed some Christian marriages coming adrift at the seams. They realistically agreed they were not "super people" and had no guarantees of being any more successful at marriage than any other of the Christians they knew; and so they built what seemed to be a commonsense safeguard into their marriage. By doing this they had built an escape clause that could lead them to accept divorce too easily, and not to fight to build the kind of marriage which grows strong only as it survives the stresses and strains of testing through which all good marriages pass.

But who can blame the wife who escapes from home as fast as possible to the world of work in today's world? Life has changed, and women who now are at home all day tend to be incredibly lonely and isolated. Terraced houses and tight-knit communities are becoming history – they hardly exist today among high-rise dwellings or "keep-yourself-to-yourself commuterland". No longer can the wife at home chat to the neighbours as she hangs out her laundry in the garden. The village grocer and the corner shop, where you could go in the past and pretend you'd run out of tea when really you wanted someone to chat to for half an hour, have been swallowed up in most places by the "super and hyper" and "bigger and better" and more computerized and less personal stores.

Increasing mobility in today's society and the expectation that every promotion for the husband involves moving house and living in another part of the country, means that few wives live in the communities where they are well known and know others well. Many families move every few years, making it impossible to build lasting friendships. Few families live near their own relatives. If a wife is lonely she can no longer pop into Mum's for a cuppa – for Mum probably lives two hundred miles up the M1 and is as inaccessible as if she was on the moon. Where there are provisions for pre-school children in crèches, playgroups or mother-and-toddler clubs, these are often so limited that relatively few mothers have access to them.

Even a visitor to the house must now be regarded with suspicion until proved harmless. Today's mother has to assume that the friendly man who comes to read the gas meter, or the young woman selling flowers, cannot be trusted. They may be from one of the cults, a confidence trickster or a mugger. This means that visitors from local churches, who genuinely may be seeking out the lonely to try to befriend them, do not have easy access to homes or a ready welcome. In our age where mugging, rape and theft appear increasingly common, fear has become one of the greatest factors leading to increased loneliness for young wives at home.

The dramatic increase in the numbers of sleeping pills and tranquillizers prescribed, and the recent phenomenon of physical addiction to these medicines, has become an eloquent but silent witness to the loneliness and insecurity felt by many women in today's society. Between 20 and 35 per cent of mothers who are alone at home with young children suffer from serious depression.[2]

For many women, a job outside the home can provide the answer to their needs. But confusion and tension can result if the implications of this are not properly thought through from a biblical perspective.

Alice, a vicar's wife, explained: "I could no longer accept that God intended me to be no more than an extension of my husband's ministry and to be the unpaid curate in Bob's parish. God had given me distinct gifts of my own which weren't being used until I started a job outside home and away from the parish."

For Sylvia, home was "restricting and boring. Until I went out to work I didn't feel whole as a person."

Many Christian married women have broken with tradition and entered the working world with little thought. Perhaps few have tried to assess in depth what might be the very best for the marriage and their children, and to discover what *God* wanted them to do. The subject has provoked little discussion from the pulpit. The basic question should surely be asked: Is it right for wives and mothers to be working or not?

Since the older generation of Christian wives tended not to work outside home, there are few for those of us who now work to observe, to model ourselves on, and to learn from. So far only a few have blazed the trail and successfully combined motherhood, building a secure marriage and home, and nurturing their children in Christ, with a career. Therefore, it is largely my generation of Christian working women who are making the mistakes (plenty of them), learning what to do and not to do, and providing a pattern for the future.

For those not trained to think and ask questions, it has seemed easiest simply to follow the pattern set out by secular society without going through a period of soul-searching: "What is right for me, my husband, and family – and above all what do I understand from the Bible that God is trying to say to me about this?"

The Christian couple from a conservative evangelical background may face problems in their marriage if the wife works outside the home which seem almost unbelievable to those in secular society. Those who intend to live in obedience to biblical teaching read the words: "Wives submit to your husbands as to the Lord. For the husband is the head of the wife as Christ is the head of the Church, his body, of which he is the Saviour. Now as the Church is subject to Christ, so also wives should submit to their husbands in everything" (Ephesians 5: 22–24).

This is interpreted in all kinds of different ways. There are some husbands who feel that they cannot "control" their wives if they go out to work. Sometimes this has more to do with their own insecurity as husbands, than with what the Bible really teaches. Such men need to examine their motives carefully; some will find that they are asking their wives not to threaten their male egos by combining homemaking with a career outside the home.

If a wife has been at home all the time the children were little and suddenly goes out to work, the transition from kitchen to office may make her blossom and grow as a person; her husband may not know how to react and may feel threatened.

The wife whose sole topic of conversation seemed to be babies and measles, schools and supermarkets, may suddenly develop an interest in, and increasing knowledge of current affairs, politics and social concerns – leaving her husband behind, plodding his familiar rut. In her enthusiasm at the opening up of her horizons after years of nappies, weaning, and school rounds, she may be insensitive to her husband's vulnerability and compound his problem by failing to stop and listen to (what is now to her) his dull day's events.

If the couple has always tried to allow the husband to be the "head" of the wife, and interpreted this as meaning that the wife makes few decisions on her own, then it can be hard for them to adjust when the wife is making decisions at work that have far greater effects than the small ones she is supposed to refer to him at home. For many this whole area has had to be reworked and rethought in mid-marriage.

In a marriage the power is usually held by the one who controls the family finances. When the wife also becomes a wage-earner this shifts the balance of power, and can cause stress and disruption. I was one of those wives who grew up accepting the traditional pattern that a husband was the breadwinner and a wife's role was loving and nurturing family members. I assumed that the man of the house had the final say in matters of importance, and that he carried out all negotiations with the big world outside home. Therefore, I assumed that things like dealing with the bank, buying a car or a house all *had* to be done by the husband. In retrospect I think that this was the teaching both of the general society in which I grew up, and of the specific church circle in which I moved.

I saw my role as that of bearing and bringing up our children, and generating and sustaining love in our family. It seemed important to me to try to boost my husband's "headship" by never stepping out of line, and by behaving as I thought I was expected to. However, the lives John and I actually led were contradictions to the way in which I assumed I was supposed to be living.

As John was a busy surgeon, responsible also for the running of a mission hospital, it was important for his time away from the hospital to be given to his children. Therefore, it made sense for me to shoulder the responsibility for family budgeting and working out how best the money would go round. As a practical arrangement it worked well at times for me to carry certain loads to free John for other more "important" things – as long as he had the final right to say "no" if something I had thought of doing wasn't what he really wanted. But somewhere inside myself I had a nagging feeling that this system that worked so well for us might be wrong. I imagined preachers proclaiming: "Women should stay at home and let their men deal with the outside world as God ordained it to be in his structure of authority. Woman is under the man and must remain in her subordinate position . . ."

Popular, so-called "Christian" teaching has confused some Christian couples, and led them into a mindless, blind following of a pattern which is passed off as biblical but which is questionable and certainly cannot be taught with authority as being God's set pattern for all mankind.

Within both the evangelical Christian world and society generally, the Christian couple may find it is difficult to discern God's pattern for marriage today. When I qualified as a doctor twenty-five years ago, it was in the era when women doctors were beginning to be accepted as equal to their male counterparts. At work I was expected to carry the same case-load as a man, to be able to assess patients accurately and to make life-and-death decisions. It therefore made no sense if, when I was at home, others expected me to be incapable of making even the smallest and most insignificant decisions. In the end, it was freely giving my husband the final say and the right to veto what I thought was the best way to do things, that was my personal expression of his God-given "headship".

I had to part company with those Christians who expected me as a wife to act the part of a dumb idiot, unable to think for herself, who looked sweet and parroted her husband's words without being able to express an opinion of her own. To me, this was dishonest and hypocritical. And, as one who followed the Lord Jesus Christ, who declared himself to be "the Truth", how could I live a lie and pretend to be other than the person he had made me to be?

Reaching this point in my life did not spare me the self-doubt and the heart-searching of feeling that I might somehow be disobeying God by failing to conform to the expectations of the narrow segment of the Church in which I happened to be involved at the time, and whose opinion was important to me. It was years later that I could look back and see that my tension and feeling of discomfort were largely due to my not having thought through secular marriage patterns or related them to my understanding of what the Bible taught.

I have not found it necessary to adopt what I see as some of the extremes of the feminist movement. I do not have natural aggressive or violent feelings about men. Nor do I really want to take full charge of my life and live independently of my husband. The New Testament and the Lord Jesus teach that in Christ there is neither "male nor female". The Lord Jesus Christ honoured women, and did not treat them as inferior to men.

My worth, as a woman, in God's eyes is no more and no less than the worth of a man. The fact that he has created me to be different from a man in no way diminishes my value to him. Therefore, I expect other Christians to treat me in the way that God does — as a person created in his image and precious to him. Whether I happen to be male or female does not matter greatly.

Christianity is essentially about relationships — primarily those between God and man, but also those between man and man, and man and woman. Anything that enhances the quality of those relationships should, I believe, be important to a Christian.

Chapter 3

After three decades, two of my friends have reached a stage in their marriage where it is clear that they have not only managed to stay together, but that they have really loved one another all these years. However, only a few people have known them long enough to realize that in the beginning it looked as if everything was weighted against them.

They came from separate remote villages in Thailand, and their marriage had been arranged by their parents. Although they met beforehand, they hardly knew one another. For family reasons each willingly agreed to marry the other. At first they were polite, fulfilling what was expected of them. Then they began to talk and to share with one another, and to see life from the other's perspective. As the years passed, mutual respect developed and gradually changed into the calibre of love that survives life's normal stresses and crises.

Their marriage was far less complicated than that of today's Western bride and groom, for each expected far less of the other than a wedding couple in the UK now expects. Their entire lives were far more risky than ours in our Welfare State. The most important matters in their lives included cultivating the rice in their family paddy fields and stopping it from being eaten by pests or destroyed by drought. Life was about tending the family's water buffaloes so that they were strong enough to pull the ploughs, tread the grain, and drag the grain-laden carts back from the fields. Destruction of crops or loss of buffaloes spelt potential disaster for a family. When life is lived at a basic level like this, then expectations of marriage are far more fundamental than we in the West can afford.

This is explained by Dr Jack Dominian: "When the basic needs of survival are reached, human beings imperceptibly seek fulfilment at a deeper level of their being, where the world of feelings, emotions and sexuality are engaged. Both sexes, but particularly women, expect more in the way of fulfilment at this level." [1]

Few couples in Britain are fighting for mere survival for themselves and their children, as many do in the Third World. We grumble – rightly or wrongly – that we pay too much tax, the rates are too high, the DHSS treats us badly, that the dole, child benefit, supplementary benefit etc. are too low when our lifestyle is not as luxurious as we think it should be. Yet, comparing our lives with those of couples in other parts of the world, where a radio is a luxury, where one pair of shoes is shared by several family members, where toothpaste cannot be afforded, then we begin to sense that our times of misfortune might, to people like them, appear as times of unprecedented luxury.

A sad sequel to Western prosperity is that as a nation we have tended to concentrate on materialism and to forfeit our spiritual heritage. Spiritual values have been lost in the quest to acquire more and more things. We build our homes like small palaces and live isolated from our neighbours. In other parts of the world, where survival is the name of the game, the fittest, cleverest and strongest fight for the survival of themselves and of those who are theirs. The tough go forward, and the weak go under. It is hardly surprising that marriage in such a culture is seen differently from marriage in modern Britain.

Couples who do not have to struggle merely to survive are couples who are likely to possess the potential and the energy which makes it possible to develop a unique relationship in marriage – of fully developing their husband and wife relationship. Postwar rising standards of living in Britain have changed the quality of relationship that couples today generally feel they have a right to expect from their marriage partner.

It now seems that when John and I fell in love, we were like characters in sentimental, romantic paperback novels. I floated above the dissecting rooms in the medical school studying anatomy, seeing each lifeless body as a creation of extreme and rare beauty. I did not notice the formalin preservative that made the room reek and my eyes smart – instead I imagined the scent of spring flowers and heard birds singing in the lecture halls. When John asked me if I would marry him once I had qualified as a doctor, my reply was an unhesitating "Yes!"

We were in love and that was all that mattered to us. I wanted, and expected, little more from life than to marry John, be with him, bear and rear his children, and to serve God with John wherever that was to be. We both expected to stay together "till death us do part" – and, in those days, divorce was so rare that it never crossed our minds.

During my twenty-five years of marriage, life in Britain has changed. The standard of living has risen considerably, and I – along with many others – have changed in my expectation of marriage. Where once I expected to be committed to my partner for life, and little more, I now find that I am looking for a relationship with my marriage partner that is deeper and more meaningful than any other human relationship. Being children of our times, many of us Christians find that our expectations of marriage have changed in parallel with those in secular society.

I believe that this particular change in thinking could have a positive effect on many Christian marriages, and therefore welcome it. Instead of marriage being a somewhat sterile existence for some couples, with very clearly defined roles of husband as breadwinner and wife as homemaker, it is shifting towards a deeper, more loving and more understanding relationship between couples. This is in keeping with the priority that the Lord Jesus Christ continually places on the way that people relate to one another. Everything that happens in secular society is not automatically wrong or detrimental! Because today's society emphasizes the importance of the quality of the relationship of husband and wife, Christians can recognize this as a reflection of God's image in man – God who *is* relationship. Whether man knows his Creator or not, in his yearning for a deeper marriage relationship he is reflecting his Creator's character. Intimate, trusting relationships lie at the heart of the Godhead – where Father, Son and Spirit commune in the mystery of the Holy Trinity. Man, created in God's image, reflects some of the divine attributes and will never attain that for which God made him unless he lives in close communion with both God and with another person, or people. And, as Dr Jack Dominian comments: "No one comes to know himself through introspection, or in the solitude of a personal diary. Rather, it is in dialogue, in his meetings with other persons. It is only by expressing his convictions to others that he becomes really conscious of them." [2]

Surveys in America in 1984 indicated that college students are shifting away from the permissive attitudes of the last couple of decades in which sexual expression was thought natural and normal for any two people (of different or the same sex) who have sexual desires for one another. Instead, students are apparently beginning to reverse this trend, and are seeking as a sexual partner someone with whom they have a relationship involving some degree of permanence and commitment. Experience has taught them that former generations of students found neither the total bliss nor the absolute fulfilment that the so-called "freedom" of sexual permissiveness was supposed to give them. Rather, in its wake, the "permissive society" has left washed up on its shore many disillusioned, empty and cynical characters, now building life on the solid foundations they missed when younger.

When God made us "in his image", he created us with a need for a lasting communion with at least one other person

– with a basic need to be understood and to understand a partner. If we fail to follow the Designer's plans, then we should not be surprised when things go wrong. Changing partners (no matter for what reason) is not what God intended when he created us. We function best when we learn to live in the security of close friendship and commitment to one other person.

The fact that this was God's original intention for mankind (before man fell in the Garden of Eden) is important, since many interpret this as indicating it to be God's ideal for all men and women, for all time, for all situations, regardless of race, religion or culture. (They would refer to it technically as a "creation ordinance".)

In the Bible's clear words we read: "Then the Lord God said, 'It is not good for the man to live alone. I will make a suitable companion to help him.' . . . He formed a woman out of the rib and brought her to him. Then the man said, 'At last, here is one of my own kind – bone taken from my bone, and flesh from my flesh. "Woman" is her name because she was taken out of man.' That is why a man leaves his father and mother and is united with his wife, and they become one. The man and the woman were both naked, but they were not embarrassed" (Genesis 2:18, 22–24, GNB).

Despite protest from those who feel that life is giving them a raw deal (having myself lived for sixteen years in a Third World country), I feel that we in Britain can hardly be said to be battling for survival. We have the luxury (not available to others in other parts of the world) of being able to concentrate quite a lot of time and energy on working at building the calibre of husband-wife relationship which God intends us to experience.

Yet, many middle-aged couples today are trapped in a land of in-between. As children, they grew up during or just after the war, when parents were struggling with coupons and ration books to feed and clothe their children, and had little energy to build up the relationship at the heart of the family – that between husband and wife. Therefore, some middle-aged couples have not seen a pattern of marriage in their parents' lives which gives them a model of a close relationship to copy – perhaps their parents' marriage was more like that of a good working partnership. The way we behave as husband and wife is usually modelled on that which we unconsciously learn from watching our own parents. If our parents were struggling to bring us up, then they may not have shown us the pattern of two people who share deeply, and so we may not have concepts built into our thinking and emotional life that will enable us easily to form deep relationships with one other person.

Some of us discover that we have developed into adults who find it easier to live a life of solitude rather than to share ourselves with others. Friends at school and during childhood were simply those with whom we associated when we "ran with the pack". Our adult relationships may be with those with whom we associate at work or at church. We may assume we have satisfactory relationships and may appear to have many friends – when reality reveals these to be shallow and superficial. Close scrutiny may show that some have no close friends to whom everything can be unburdened, nor a desire for any such people. Someone like this presents a problem to his or her marriage partner.

I believe that the seemingly self-sufficient person is deprived of one of the richest and most important things which God intended to build into our lives – the ability to be known and of knowing, and through this of fully finding ourselves as human beings. The Lord Jesus Christ, God's Son, when on earth expressed his dependence on his Father. His example encourages us to develop our closeness with others. Speaking of his relationship with the Father, Jesus says: "I do nothing on my own . . ." (John 8:28).

Current popular psychology teaches us that people are made for people, and that healthy relationships are vital for our full development. Couples entering marriage today will usually have far higher expectations of one another in this way than former generations did. It is likely that both, or at least one of them, will expect deeper, honest sharing, more openness and greater conscious oneness than was expected by older married couples. Those who fail to experience their expectations may feel cheated, disillusioned, and bitterly disappointed. Society now makes it easy to take the option of divorce as the way of escape from a marriage which does not come up to those high standards of intimacy. Easy divorce suggests this is a better option than the harder one of working through the pain to build a strong, mature and deep relationship.

When I married, I did not expect John to understand me to the degree which I now expect. It is obvious to me that my thinking and expectations have been changed by the society in which I live, and the cultural values that I have absorbed through the media. These values are also being taught by some churches in America and have come over to Britain in American books about Christian marriage. The importance of relationship is gradually being taught by the Church here in Britain, as marriage-encounter and marriage-enrichment courses are increasingly being encouraged by churches.

I find now that I want my husband to understand all that there is to know about me. I don't want any part of me to be hidden – even my secret hurts and vulnerability. Armed with such understanding, I want him to anticipate certain things that will cause me pain. But I need to realize that such a demand is probably unrealistic – the *media* have taught me first to want him to know these things and then to expect him to know them intuitively, without my even telling him.

Therefore, watching the television news at night, I realize that I now almost expect John to have cottoned on to the fact that during the day certain things have conspired to put me in a certain frame of mind. I then expect him to know that a news item about refugees will upset me more that night than it normally would. And I begin to expect him to sense whether or not I want to sit in silence in the moonlit garden praying through my pain to the One who carried the suffering of the world on the cross, or whether I need something totally different – John's strong arms round me, a shoulder on which to weep, followed by a strong cup of tea and a good laugh. Yes, I am expecting too much – and he and I both know it!

I expect a husband to know intuitively when I am moved by compassion at the plight of the helpless, or with righteous indignation that certain injustices should be allowed to continue unchanged in the perfect world God created. I expect a husband to sense the heartbeat of my emotions – to feel my joy, to know my moods, enter my feelings, and never strangle moments of pure, silent pleasure with mundane words like "Penny for your thoughts". Of course, I expect him to notice when I'm in a bad temper but, more than that, I want him to know without being told when the cause of it is premenstrual tension, or worry about money, or anxiety about one of the children, or sheer exhaustion or chronic illness.

The older I get, the more I seem to expect! Like an open book I want my husband to read me and understand not only what I say but what lies behind the words, so that he hears each one of my unspoken communications. But with increasing age comes the wisdom of realizing that I expect more than is humanly possible, and no matter what the media say about modern marriage, it is rare that any couple attains the quality of relationship they might have been led to expect is their *right*. My expectations and longings are quite different from those I had (or rather, did not have) when we entered marriage. With hindsight, I see that I expect from my marriage partner something that is unrealistic and unfair.

In talking to other wives, I discover I am not alone. Others, too, have been swept up by what is implied or taught in magazines, papers, books and on the TV, and some feel that their marriage has failed for not being what it "ought to be". Sadly, few of those who think their marriage has failed have stopped on the way to the divorce courts and asked: "Am I expecting too much?"

Society today may lead us to expect what is unattainable by the average couple and we need to accept this. But we also need to understand not only ourselves, but also the differences that exist between some men and some women.

I, in keeping with many other women, do not find it difficult to express openly my fears with someone with whom I feel safe. If I know that this person will accept me despite the things in me which I see as weakness and for which I despise myself, then I find it brings both relief and healing to share these fears with that person. Typical men, on the other hand, usually find it far harder to be open about their fears with anyone.

For a husband to share with his wife some of the vulnerable areas of himself, in which he possibly feels he may be a "failure" or may be "weak", can be incredibly difficult. The fear of being judged and of being criticized if weakness is allowed to surface, lurks deep. It is very hard for some men to dare to reveal areas of possible failure to a wife or close friends, from whom they long for affirmatory words of admiration and encouragement. How much easier to maintain an outward façade that all is well than to allow a crack to appear in an impenetrable exterior, which could open up interior reality and expose vulnerability. The price of being real with one's spouse may seem too costly (in terms of the risk of rejection) to make it worth experimenting with. Yet no deep human relationship can exist and grow unless couples learn to share honestly the things about which they are most ashamed.

To remove my outward veneer of protective covering and to show my partner some of the painful areas of myself is not easy. It is far easier to hide behind the smooth, happy, glossy exterior than to run the risk of revealing myself, finding that my partner rejects me for what I have shown, fails to understand the implications of what has been shared, takes my words and uses them at some future date to wound me deliberately or thoughtlessly, or simply laughs at me for being childish.

Relationships that are of value are usually achieved through the pain of working through misunderstanding, misinterpretation, self-revelation and all the risks involved, and the vulnerability of exposing oneself to another person. But I believe that these are the relationships that really count, and that the one relationship that is central in the lives of most of us – that of marriage – is the one which deserves all we can possibly invest in it.

Many of us protect *ourselves* by criticizing our partner, by nagging and finding fault. Many of us need to ask God to give us the self-control that will stop destructive words that can never be taken away once they have been uttered. We need to understand that often criticism of a partner is a defence mechanism to protect ourselves from being judged and found wanting. Unless we learn to make our partner feel accepted, we cannot expect openness from our partner. Until each feels safe with the other and knows that even the worst that is shared can never take away the love and total support of the other person, he or she may feel unable to share those things that go deepest and which most need to be brought out into the open.

Another fear faced by men is, as Paul Tournier explains: "that of receiving advice ... the husband began by unveiling his anxieties, but, in the face of such ready-made answers, he withdraws. He is crushed in the hope before being able to show his wife all the aspects of a delicate problem. The wife's intention was good but she ruined everything by replying too quickly. She should have listened longer and tried to understand."[3]

He goes on to underline the fact that often a husband and wife need to learn to listen to one another, to really hear what is being said, and to remain silent in understanding. We fail to realize that the advice we give in trying to be helpful may be counterproductive and have the opposite effect to that intended. It may be received by the defeated thought of our spouse: "I knew I wasn't much good at that – and what's being said just now shows how wrong I get it every time I try. Why go on . . . ?" Advice given at the wrong time and in the wrong way can be just as hurtful as direct criticism.

If we are going to deepen our understanding of our partner, as I believe most of us need to do if we are to have the marriage God intends for us, then we need to learn how to listen. For many couples this means creating the space and the place for real sharing to go on. It isn't enough after the supper washing-up to mutter casually, "How was today?" as part of the routine timetable into which many families settle. Real sharing means a couple creatively building the right atmosphere in which each partner can relax and be free from other distractions, to talk about the deep things that get pushed down even deeper in the business of life.

Some busy couples find it necessary to book an evening for one another weekly in their diaries – keeping the date sacrosanct. Others find it good to go out regularly for a meal together. Others find that locking the teenagers out of the bedroom for half an hour is what they need. It takes time and trouble to develop a relationship. Yet, sadly, few married couples give their own relationship any place on their list of priorities, let alone place number two under God.

Having found the time and place to share, we then need to learn how to listen. We need to learn to discard our feelings of negativity – "Not that again – I've heard it all before and I'm sick of it . . ."; "That's so wrong . . . it's time it was stopped . . ."; "If it was me then I'd have done it differently and I'm sure it would have worked out better . . ." These feelings may not be openly expressed but are sometimes communicated by attitude or tone of voice and can kill any real sharing once, and possibly, for all.

Paul Tournier explains:

> Deep sharing is overwhelming and very rare. A thousand fears keep us in check . . . the fear of breaking down, of crying; that the other will not sense the importance with which this feeling or memory is charged . . . How painful it is when such a difficult sharing falls flat either on ears too preoccupied or mocking, ears that in any case do not sense the tremendous significance of what we are saying. It may happen between a man and wife. The partner who has spoken in a very personal way without being understood falls back into terrible emotional solitude. It is impossible to overemphasize the immense need men have to be really listened to, to be understood. No one can develop freely in this world and find a full life without feeling understood by at least one person. Misunderstood, he loses his self-confidence, he loses his faith in life or even in God.[4]

The "me" that is here at the end of the 1980s wants to understand my husband and to be totally understood. I can do this when John looks at me with the eyes of real love – the love that accepts me as I am without condemnation or judgement. Not saying that evil is good, but saying: "I love you despite that weakness. I'll help you face it anyway, don't feel alone with it. Let's carry it together and overcome it together . . ."

But the young "me" that first married twenty-five years ago, had not yet learned that it could be safe to share my inner self with any other person, nor had I then anticipated that I could ever understand another person deeply. It is hard for married couples of my generation to be told that it is now safe to express emotions, to cry in front of another, to display anger or aggression, guilt, jealousy or hurt. But until we share our inner selves like this, we fail to benefit from the good that current culture has shown us – that a married couple can be close emotionally and mentally as well as physically.

To strip off the outward veneer that has stuck firmly with each year that has passed is painful – but, like some surgery, it is worth the price of pain. It is not too late for many of us "young middle-aged" couples to begin again and to relate to one another in a deeper and closer way – provided we are prepared to work for it, and to run the risk of being vulnerable to hurt.

Chapter 4

A few years ago, I read the book *A Severe Mercy* written by Sheldon Vanauken, a protégé of someone I greatly respect, C. S. Lewis. On the one hand, their writing filled me with exquisite joy that the taste of nuptial union and communion could be so sweet and rich to any couple, yet on the other hand it filled me with the blackest of frustrated and hopeless despair, and unmet yearning. "God, it's not fair!" I angrily prayed. "Why have you overwhelmed this couple with so much exceptional love for each other and left the rest of us to plod on in marriages that take so much work and effort . . . ?"

It was as if God gently tapped me on the shoulder and explained: "You've all your life to learn how to be the wife I have designed you to be . . . the woman in that book had only a short time with her husband before she died. I wanted their marriage to be a living picture to others of what Christian marriage could be like – a picture of Jesus being the bridegroom of the Church . . ." (see Ephesians 5:31–33).

There that couple stood in the pages of their book, with their intuitive awareness of one another's needs and complete absorption in each other – apparently, totally loving and absolutely understanding. In contrast, there were John and I at that time – missionary doctors in Thailand – slogging our hearts out to bring healing in Christ's name to those who were desperately ill. That book's portrait of an "ideal" marriage, and the mundane reality of marriages around me, stood in sharp contrast – and I must confess that at times I was jealous.

I do not believe – except in moments of great selfishness –

that God intends me to be grasping to find absolute fulfilment and complete satisfaction for all my emotional needs from my husband. I'd like to find some of these met. But I believe it is more the teaching of the society in which we live than that of God's Word, that leads me to expect to discover self-fulfilment, complete understanding, and have every need met in my marriage partner.

Just looking at those words is enough to show me how ridiculous such an idea is for a Christian. Yet such thinking has crept into some Christian writing in the last decade. Our concept of marriage has been infiltrated by ideas that are derived from the world and not from the Bible. For the Christian, happiness and self-fulfilment are not God's be-all and end-all in life – far from it. Hedonism and Christianity are incompatible; they are mutually exclusive opposites.

It is in the affirmation that a search for happiness is not what life is really about, that many Christians have had to rethink and re-evaluate their marriages. In doing this they inevitably stumble and stub their toes on words obnoxious to most twentieth-century couples – words like "headship", "submission", and "authority". It is here that the Christian married couple may find itself standing against the tide of popular opinion – sometimes swimming with the crowd, sometimes being submerged by a massive wave and then humbly returning to God, repenting that the things that have gone wrong are because the couple took society's values and teaching as a pattern for marriage, rather than biblical principles. Many norms for life today in secular society stand in stark contrast to that which the Bible depicts as the normal way in which Jesus' followers should live.

If we look at our partners and automatically expect them to be the means by which all our legitimate needs are met, then most of us face inevitable disappointment and run into trouble. It is easy then to say: "She's not what I need in a wife any more, so I'm off . . ." It becomes as simple to discard the one who should be a life partner as it is to lightly throw away anything no longer of use in our disposable society.

But God does not dispose of people when apparently they are of no use to him. He hangs on to people who are failures – like Peter, who denied him three times – and transforms them into disciples whom he will use to build his Church. I believe that God intends us to hang on to our marriage partners – especially when failure is written large over our relationships. The God who does not give up on us, does not intend us to give up on our partners just because we feel a marriage has "failed" to a greater or lesser degree. God neither gives up on us, nor does he abandon his intention to weld us together so tightly that nothing short of death can wrench us apart – for we are inextricably woven together into what in God's eyes is an indivisible oneness.

When the dream has faded, when the honeymoon is well and truly over, and when marriage is at its most boring, then the Christian must dig his heels into the ground and refuse to give up. For this is likely to be the make-or-break point for his marriage.

Along with Helmut Thielicke, he must deliberately dismiss any thoughts that either happiness or self-fulfilment can be raised to the rank "of being the real mark of a full life". Thielicke goes on to say:

> To achieve self-realization, to realize one's optimal potentialities and to "use" the other person to that end threatens the destiny of a dethroned god who seems to be staging his comeback in a secularized world.
>
> When [a partner] no longer satisfies those claims – because of age, the deadening power of familiarity or boredom etc. – he is dismissed. I no longer deal with him as a person with the "infinite value of a human soul"; I value him only for what he is worth . . . [a person] whose importance to me stands or falls as he performs or does not perform his functions for me. There is no room here

for *agape* love, which lives not by making claims on but by giving, and which by loving makes the other person worth loving.[1]

As partners, a married couple hold in their hands the awesome ability of encouraging the development of each other to God's full potential – or, they can crush and annihilate that into which the other might blossom given the right climate in marriage.

In a world where confusion reigns as to the value and role of women, the Christian wife may find herself bewildered and uncertain of who she is and what she should be. She is most likely to assert loudly that the day of the stern authoritarian husband, whose slippers must be warmed and placed on his feet after work, who must be fed before women and children, and whose word is equivalent to God's command to her, was destroyed in the bombs of the last two world wars which brought a measure of liberation to women.

Her Christian sisters do exist in small numbers in isolated pockets in Britain, convinced that they grievously disobey God if they venture out to the supermarket without their husband's "covering" permission. But they form a minority. Some of them actually believe their husband's unspoken thoughts: "I and my wife are one – and I am that one." Words like these are not a joke to them.

Today, Christian women in their thousands regard marriage as a partnership of equals. They and their husbands believe that he has no more say in the dynamics of that relationship and its practical outworking than she does. Such a marriage pattern is easier to accept in society today, when women have more opportunities in life and are accorded greater respect in the secular world than before.

If we are to understand how biblical principles relate to women in today's marriages, then it helps us if we can begin to grasp what was happening to marriage at the time when

Jesus was alive, and when the early Church was giving its basic teaching on marriage which appears in the epistles.

Two major cultures, Roman and Greek, affected the way in which people regarded the status of women and their place in marriage at that time. Both had pervaded attitudes and influenced thought patterns. Our raised eyebrows today on hearing how women were seen is a credit to Christianity and the way its teachings have shaped Western thinking. In the time of Jesus, according to Becker, women were regarded as a "lower order of beings, neglected by nature in comparison with man. This was both on the point of intellect and heart – they were incapable of taking part in public life, naturally prone to evil, and fitted only for propagating the species and gratifying the appetites of men . . ."

Apparently, the Greeks commonly said: "We keep mistresses for pleasure; we keep prostitutes for the day-to-day needs of the body; we keep wives to bear our legitimate children and to be the faithful guardians of our homes."

William Barclay explains:

In his very beautiful essay, "Precepts for Wives", Plutarch draws a picture of marriage as a fellowship in which all is shared and in which the words "mine" and "yours" never occur, for everything is "ours".

But in the same essay he actually justifies the Greek way of life by suggesting that a man in using a prostitute pays his wife a compliment by making others the instrument of his passion and sparing her the experience. There are few statements which throw so revealing a light on the position of the Greek wife.[2]

Classical Greek society contained a unique group of women called the *hetari*, the "companions". They were the most brilliant, most accomplished and most highly educated women of their day. Opening their salons, it was they who posed the greatest threat to marriages – for the level of intelligent friendship they provided for men was something that no ordinary wife could hope to offer.

Barclay continues:

> The situation in Greece is completely extraordinary. In the nature of things, the Greek wife could hardly be a companion for her husband; it involved no stigma at all for a man to find satisfaction outside his marriage bond, and it was often with that extraordinary and brilliant race of *hetari* that men found their real fellowship.
>
> There were happy marriages in Greece . . . Among the humbler people there was much more fidelity. But it is also true that among the upper classes, at the time when Christianity was emerging, marriage was very near to breaking down completely.

At this time, Roman marriage was taken more seriously than in Greece. However, as Barclay reflects sadly: "Rome had conquered Greece, but Greek morals had conquered Roman." Into Roman marriages came changes for the worse. "A kind of revulsion against marriage" is Barclay's description. It heralded an age of almost universal sexual permissiveness outside marriage, which swept across the country. Not only was prostitution widespread, but the use of prostitutes was regarded not only as normal but also as something which no sensible person would object to. "An age of utter shamelessness about immoral conduct . . . and incredible coarse shamelessness . . ." are Barclay's words.

The consequence of such breakdown in marital fidelity was a massive break-up of marriage itself, and a soaring rise in the divorce rate. "The moral problems of our own time are far from new. The fact that they are not new does not make them any less serious, but it does remind us that

Christianity is not facing anything which it was not called to face before . . ." Barclay comments.

Talking to Andrew, while I was writing this, I realized how much contemporary British culture has in common with the society in which Jesus lived. And that makes Jesus' teachings especially relevant for us today.

When I first met Andrew, he had managed to get his life into about as much of a mess as anyone can. It showed in his obvious weight loss, haggard face and eyes that filled quickly with tears: "I'm desperate." The voice was unsteady. "I want to stay with my wife and children but I can't seem to avoid being involved with other women. I got on really well with one person in our church – Betty – and we spent a lot of time together in church work . . . the inevitable happened, and our friendship developed into a full-blown affair. Betty's husband left her for someone else. Now she needs me to support her – and I accept that it's my fault that she is now on her own."

He found the next part hard to say. "But it's worse than that. Now I've really grown to love someone else, Jane, and can talk to her and share myself with her in a way that I can't with either my wife or with Betty. I know it can't go on like this. But how can I hurt both Betty and Jane by breaking completely with them – when I'm the cause of the present predicament and pain? I'm responsible for fifty per cent of what has happened between us . . . and now I'm trapped . . . whatever I do is bound to be wrong."

I suspect that Andrew would have fitted well into Greek society. He was a man who found sexual fulfilment outside marriage, and who also gained from someone other than his wife emotional and intellectual stimulation, and the fulfilment that he ought to have been deriving from his wife. But Andrew is a man of the 1980s, and the logical outcome of his course of action would probably mean that before too long his marriage could well be added to the statistic of one in three marriages that break up in today's society.

49

It was into a culture full of people playing marriage as a variation on Andrew's theme, that the Lord Jesus brought his revolutionary teaching about women – teaching alien to the spirit of the age. Not only did Jesus say extraordinary things about women, but he showed by his actions that he meant what he said. Unlike other religious teachers, Jesus indicated that women were as valuable to him as men. He loved some as friends, he spent time with them, gave them his undivided attention. They were the last at his cross and the first at his empty tomb. It was to women that he first showed himself alive and risen from the dead. Yes, women were special to Jesus!

As the New Testament teaches: "There is neither Jew nor Greek, slave nor free, male nor female, for you are all one in Christ Jesus" (Galatians 3:28). How then does the New Testament speak of marriage to a culture resembling ours today? Do we find what we expect to, or are there apparent anomalies?

At first glance, New Testament teaching on marriage may appear irrelevant and having virtually nothing to say that is helpful to the culture for which it was written. Greek and Roman wives were commonly underdogs, and therefore New Testament teaching to them to "submit" to their husbands may superficially appear to do little more than to make a bad state of affairs worse. Surely, all such wives should rise up as one and fight for the fact that "in Christ there is neither male nor female"?

How does the attitude of Jesus himself towards women square with teachings in the epistles like: "Wives submit yourselves to your husbands as to the Lord" (Ephesians 5:22), and "Wives, submit yourselves to your husbands, as is fitting in the Lord" (Colossians 3:18). Are such words at variance with Jesus and what he taught? For instance, does someone like Andrew's wife meekly "submit" and allow him to be sexually involved with Betty and to have an intense emotional attachment to Jane? All this at her expense and for his benefit alone? Is "submission" the passive permitting of almost anything by an "inferior" in deference to the "authority" of the one who is "superior"?

I am convinced that once men like Andrew grasp the real meaning of submission and their role of "headship", and are themselves determined to live in obedience to the authority of the Bible, then their marriages and their attitudes to their wives will have to change radically.

If in Christ Jesus there is "neither male nor female" and neither is superior to the other, then what is submission about? How can you submit if you are equal? Understanding this means thinking back to the beginning of our world, and how we were made.

John Stott explains:

> Sexual equality, established by the creation but perverted by the Fall, was recovered by the redemption that is in Christ.
>
> What redemption remedies is the Fall; what it recovers and re-establishes is the creation. Thus men and women are absolutely equal in their worth before God – equally created by God like God, equally justified by grace through faith, equally regenerated by the outpoured Spirit.
>
> In other words, in the new community of Jesus we are not only sharers of God's image but also equally heirs to his grace in Christ (1 Peter 3:7) and equally indwelt by his Spirit. This Trinitarian equality (our common participation in Father, Son and Holy Spirit) nothing can ever destroy. Christians and churches in different cultures have denied it; but it is an indestructible fact.[3]

So, men and women are of equal value. But equal worth does not mean that men and women share the same identity. It is part of the amazing wonder of creation that God designed both sexes so that they would complement one another through their distinctly different sexuality, psychological make-up, physiological functioning and anatomical differences. They are equal but different – equal with different functions to perform. As J. H. Joder expresses it: "Equality of worth is not identity of role."

Because a woman does not fulfil a man's role (or vice versa) it does not mean that she (or he) is of less value in God's eyes – or, theoretically, in the eyes of the Church or society. Martin Luther elucidates with this explanation:

> I have often said that we must sharply distinguish between these two, the office and the person. The man who is called Hans or Martin is a man quite different from the one who is called elector, doctor or preacher. Here we have two different persons in one man. The one is that in which we are created and born, according to which we are all alike – man, woman or child, young or old. But once we are born, God adorns and dresses you up as another person. He makes you a child and me a father, one is a master and another a servant, one a prince and another a citizen.[4]

To God, both Andrew, his wife, Betty and Jane are equally precious and unique individuals. But as a Christian, Andrew's wife is told to submit to him. Because he has broken his marriage vows and failed to be committed to her with the exclusiveness that is part of Christian marriage, Andrew's wife may well feel that she has biblical grounds for divorcing him. Jesus' teaching about divorce being permissible on the grounds of adultery may encourage her to build a new life apart from him.

Whether she stays or goes, Andrew is left with penetrating questions he must ask himself about his husbanding in the light of biblical teaching like: "Husbands, love your wives, just as Christ loved the Church and gave himself up for her" (Ephesians 5:25), and: "Husbands, in the same way be considerate as you live with your wives, and treat them with respect as the weaker partner and as heirs with you of the gracious gift of life, so that nothing will hinder your prayers . . ." (1 Peter 3:7).

The husband to whom the wife is to submit is expected in this biblical teaching to be selfless and self-giving to the partner entrusted to him by God.

Andrew's treatment of his wife is similar to that of hundreds of men in the culture for which the New Testament was originally written, as James Hurley says: "From the evidence we possess it would seem that women were often considered as inferior, not only with respect of legal rights, but also as human beings. In some cases this came to explicit expression; in others it is more inferential."[5]

While Andrew's case (though real) may seem exaggerated, the attitude he communicates through his behaviour is common to our times. It is obvious that his wife does not have priority in his thoughts, in claims on his time, energy and emotions. His apparent aim is for self-fulfilment. In other words, like people in the culture for whom the New Testament was written, he treats his wife as an "inferior human being".

Other Christian men today assume similar attitudes in less blatant and less obvious ways – communicating none the less to their wives that they are inferior and therefore should expect second-rate treatment. Christian men who adopt attitudes like this sometimes assume that their point of view is supported by Scripture. After all, they reason, the Bible clearly commands: "Wives, submit to your husbands, as is fitting in the Lord."

How can a wife submit and yet at the same time be equal to her husband? It is here that Christian couples sometimes stumble into mindless play-acting, and the wife pretends to be more of a dumb blonde than she really is. Sometimes the wife's genuine God-given gifts and capabilities are never exercised because this could imply to others that she was failing to submit to her husband (by "showing him up" through doing certain things better than he could). Sometimes wives never blossom and develop their full potential for mistaken fear of outshining their husbands and thus "undermining his authority over her". Other couples decide after thought (or never having thought it through, but because it makes for a quiet life) that submission is a subject best ignored, and that in their marriage each will work in partnership with the other to develop the maximal potential of both, and to allow the natural leader to lead where this seems the best exercise of complementary gifts.

Understanding what lies behind biblical teaching that wives are to submit to their "head" (their husband) helps us understand what the Bible is trying to communicate about the manner in which God first designed us to best operate within his given framework of marriage. Such understanding begins with studying principles laid down in the early chapters of the Bible. God has concepts to communicate about the nature of marriage in these so-called "creation ordinances" – ordinances containing principles appropriate for all mankind, for all time, and for all cultures – not exclusively for his followers.

The arguments about marriage which the Apostle Paul takes and uses in his letters are derived from seed thoughts in Genesis 2 and 3. They do not come from arguments being tossed around in the contemporary society to which he was writing. Elizabeth Catherwood explains:

Biblically, it is a matter of different roles laid down by God for man and woman from the beginning. Tragically, the Fall brought in a new dimension. In some ways, part of Eve's original sin was that she took the lead in the confrontation with the devil . . . She took over and led man into sin, and one of the solemn results was that the complementary headship of the husband turned into divine judgement, "He shall rule over you" (Genesis

3:16) . . . but mercifully the whole passage in Ephesians 5 is irradiated with the doctrine of the atonement. The wife is a picture of the Church, the bride of Christ, whom he loved so much that he died for her. "In the same way," Paul demands almost incredibly, "must a man love his wife." But what an encouragement to the wife to give her whole-hearted devotion to the one with whom she has become one flesh! The word in verse 16 which the NIV translates "respect" is stronger than the original, including as it does a sense of "fear". The AV "reverence" is perhaps nearer the mark with its feeling not of craven fear but of deference.[6]

How does reasoning like this come from Genesis? John Stott explains:

> [Paul] drew his readers' attention to the priority of creation ("Adam was formed and then Eve"), the mode of creation ("Man did not come from woman but woman from man"), and the purpose of creation ("Neither was man created for woman, but woman for man"). Thus, according to Scripture, although "Man is born of woman" and the sexes are interdependent, yet woman was made after man, out of man and for man. These three arguments cannot be haughtily dismissed . . .[7]

As the Bible says: "The Lord God made a woman from the rib he had taken out of the man, and he brought her to the man. The man said, 'This is now bone of my bones and flesh of my flesh; she shall be called "woman" (*issah*), for she was taken out of man (*is*)'" (Genesis 2:22–23).

That these three arguments are exegetically well-founded is confirmed by James Hurley:

> For the first born inherited command of resources and responsibility of leadership. When Eve was brought to

Adam for him to give her a name, he exercised his power to assign . . . a name was connected with control . . . And yet, woman was not made as an afterthought, or as a toy for man, but as his companion and fellow-worker, to share with him in the service of God and the custodial ruling of the earth.

How does this link up with the New Testament teaching by the Apostle Paul? Hurley explains:

Adam's response to the woman both stresses their unity ("bone of my bones and flesh of my flesh") and also stresses his rule over her in that he assigns her a name ("She shall be called . . ."). This stress on unity and subordination is familiar to us from the New Testament.[8]

So to God, a woman is as valuable as a man, but within marriage men and women have different and complementary roles to play. I believe that society's failure to accept biblical norms leads marriages (Christian and non-Christian) into trouble. This is to be expected. God created us to function best within a certain framework. As soon as we begin operating outside his guidelines, we place ourselves in a position of potential disaster. Those wives who fail to submit (in the true biblical sense), and those husbands who fail to give the truly biblical "headship" necessary for submission are developing their marriages into relationships that are not as God intended. Such marriages are unlikely to work out in the best interests of both parties – although they may seem expedient for a time. Long-term effects are often detrimental for the marriage relationship. In "submitting", a wife can blossom as a person, and a marriage flower to its full potential.

John and I have been married for many years, and still often disagree with one another. Surely, part of the reason

God joined us together was so that we could benefit from the different viewpoint of the other and be sharpened and refined by disagreement. On fundamentals we agree, but on matters of interpretation and practical outworkings of those basics we may well have different views. Usually this is easily reconcilable. There are matters on which we may agree to disagree because it is not necessary for us to think identically (we are, after all, two different people). There are other matters on which, with time, one may change his or her point of view and come more into line with the partner's way of thinking. Only once do I recall a major matter on which we could not agree.

That major matter was something about which it was vital that we should agree, because our future hung in the balance and, even more, the future of our children. A massively responsible decision had to be made that was likely to affect each one of the family for the rest of our lives. And yet, John and I could not agree on what was right. We spent nearly a year praying and seeking guidance about it. Different friends gave us conflicting advice – so they were of little help. It seemed that the more we asked God what he wanted us to do, the more he reinforced the different reply each thought he or she received from him. There was no way in which we could reconcile our disagreement. Either one of us was right and the other wrong, or for some reason God was giving us different guidance.

Finally, I (as the wife) put into words and action what is summed up by James Hurley:

> Not because I believe you are wiser in this matter (I don't) or more righteous, nor because I accept that you are right (because I don't or I wouldn't oppose you) but because I am a servant of God who has called me to honour your headship, I willingly yield to your decision. If I am wrong, may God show me. If you are wrong, may he give you the grace to acknowledge it and a chance to change.[9]

We followed what John believed to be right for us. We reaped the consequences of our actions, one of which was to make me the more confident that I must learn at times like this to submit to my husband ... even though the consequences of our action probably indicated him to have been in the wrong and me to have been in the right!

Psychiatrist Richard Winter sums up my feelings:

> We must respect the differences and similarities there are between men and women so that we can each help the other to be more fully human. Too often, in the past, the Church has resorted to "stereotyped roles" of men and women with little emphasis on the similarities of being human beings made in the image of God.
>
> On the other hand, there is pressure in our present culture to blur the difference completely and thus lose the sense of wonder and joy at the original creation intention of men and women being made for each other – equal but different.[10]

Chapter 5

Sarah sat on the edge of the armchair, smoothed her perfect hair, pulled her glove-like skirt over her knees and finally uttered the words she'd come to say: "All this talk about greater closeness in marriage these days – it's not like that for us – and I'm not that sure that I'd want it to change. Pete believes in giving me freedom to develop to my full potential, and to be quite honest I like it like that. At times I look at us and think, 'We're just about as close as ships that pass in the night – in bed – and that's all there is to us now.' But we rub along all right like that, and I'm not sure that I want to change . . ."

Her voice petered out. It ended on a note that was half a question and half hinted at a wistful longing for something that might be deeper in the way of a relationship. She was young. Perhaps she was too young to realize that later she might regret her failure to build her marriage along lines that would lead to a deep relationship. Too young to realize that given ten or twenty years more of the way they were living, little might be left to hold them together other than a couple of children, or just a piece of paper stating that they were man and wife.

I was sad for her, for them as a couple, and especially sad because they were both Christians. They seemed to be missing out on some of the essentials of Christian marriage – essentials that sound strange to modern secular marriage and are expressed in words charged with emotion, causing anger to some – words like "submission", "authority" and "headship".

Because Peter left Sarah to her own devices as his wife, she was missing the positive and enriching benefits that should have been part of her heritage in submitting to her husband as her head. Because in her church no one had ever taught the congregation about these distinctly Christian aspects of marriage, she and Pete had no way of knowing that they were living at a level less than the best that God had designed for them.

Sarah was a true daughter of her age. She saw life opening up widely for women at the end of the twentieth century and was grateful to be married to a man who took seriously the good things in the feminist movement and tried to free her to be fully herself.

Looking at the track record of women in society, they both agreed with the words of the Women's Liberation Workshop when it said:

> We believe that women in our society are oppressed. We are economically oppressed: in jobs we do full work for half pay, in the home we do unpaid work full time. We are commercially exploited in advertisements, television and press; legally we often have only the status of children. We are brought up to feel inadequate, educated to narrower horizons than men. This is our specific oppression as women.[1]

They were aware from television coverage of the United Nations Report in 1980 which stated that: "Women constitute half the world's population, perform nearly two thirds of its work hours, receive one tenth of the world's income and own less than one hundredth of the world's property!"

"That's hardly what you'd call fair!" Peter reacted. "At least let's be real about the world in which we live, and what's happening to men and women. I don't think that God smiles on injustice or on the exploitation of women – so let's try and get that right for you if we can."

In 1980 the *Women in Employment* study found that:

Overall, women are spending an increasing proportion of their lives in employment, although very few adopt the typical male pattern of continuous lifetime participation in the labour market. Most interruptions to women's working lives are for domestic reasons . . . Women are now returning to work more quickly after having a baby, and increasingly returning to work between births.[2]

As Sarah was exceptionally good at her work, promotion often hovered on the horizon. Once granted, there was always another rung on the ladder waiting for her to climb upwards. Peter was proud to be married to such a gifted woman. "Go on," he'd encourage her. "See that you make the best out of the life that God has given you. You'll only live once – get as high as you can, so that you'll be able to glorify God all the more and also be able to share your faith with people high up in your profession, where there aren't too many Christians."

Peter's words were spoken with a disarming genuineness, a naïvety, and a sad lack of thought as to exactly what he was encouraging her to do, and whether he really was encouraging her to do it for the reasons he was stating. They had both heard such reasons before. They had both heard them parroted and bandied about by older Christians. Both had unconsciously gained the impression that in order to succeed as a Christian it was important to succeed at work – success measured in terms of the quality of a marriage relationship was something about which they had never heard.

They identified with what they read about gifted career wives:

Marital difficulties can often occur among managerial women because of the conflicts between home and work. Many of the women we interviewed complained of fatigue and feelings of conflict, which resulted from running both a home and a career. Many husbands, though, were supportive in terms of their managerial wives' careers; they shared the home duties; but in reality most of the married women executives believed that they spent more hours a week on housework and child care than did their husbands. Some women, on the other hand, received no help whatsoever from their husbands in the home. Problems can also arise when a woman overtakes her husband in terms of salary and status.[3]

As far as Sarah and Peter were concerned, babies were not an option at that stage in their lives. "Later," they said, "when we've got more settled and when Sarah has reached the place in her career structure where she can take time off without missing opportunities that might never occur again."

A study of biographies written in the USA since 1962 confirms what was happening to Sarah and Peter: "Although the eminent men studied usually had children, almost 60 per cent of the women were childless. And only seven of 82 women studied had sustained a lasting marriage and children as well as a distinguished career."[4]

Among those eminent women who have been unable to sustain both a brilliant career and a marriage, and who regretfully have had to separate from their husbands, are Elizabeth Arden, Indira Gandhi, Golda Meir and Helena Rubenstein.[5]

"At least I'm not going to be anything exceptionally brilliant!" Sarah laughed. "But it would be stupid to have a baby now or I'll lose my next promotion . . ." And so they put off trying for a baby for another few years.

Peter had watched his mother serve the family and give her life to them in what seemed to be a thankless grey blur of endless domesticity, fetching and carrying for men who expected much and gave virtually nothing in return. "It won't be like that for Sarah," he had vowed to himself. "I love her and want her to be the best that God wants her to be – so I'll see she isn't tied to house and kids until it's the right time . . ."

He encouraged her to go on a course that was

> . . . designed to help women who feel they are too passive, too aggressive or too manipulative. It explains how to be assertive instead. It is about basic patterns of behaviour and how to change them . . . [women's] experience of the changing world of the past decade has taught them that they need no longer sit quietly in the back seat, but they have not yet learned to move forwards . . . to think for themselves, to speak out, to stand their ground. What they want and find in these workshops are techniques to help them handle difficult personal, professional and social situations . . . assertiveness techniques.[6]

Sarah had no Christian friends who were thinking about such matters with whom she could talk things through from a Christian perspective. Something within her cried out for justice and equality, but something else seemed to nag at her that she had not got everything quite right. What was being preached from the pulpit about family life did not always square up with life as she knew it in the business world. Sermons about marriage said next to nothing about the struggles that were facing the men and women with whom she was working. Their problems were articulated – if in a somewhat exaggerated manner – by men like Alvin Toffler in his book *The Third Wave*:

> From the day that Betty Frieden's bombshell book *The Feminine Mystique* launched the modern feminist movement in many nations, we have seen a painful struggle to redefine roles of men and women in terms appropriate to the post-nuclear family future. The

expectations and behaviour of both sexes have shifted with respect to jobs, legal and financial rights, household responsibilities, and even sexual performance.

"Now," writes Peter Knobler, editor of *Crawdaddy*, a rock-music magazine, "a guy's got to be content with women breaking all the rules . . . many regulations need breaking," he adds, "but that doesn't make it much easier."

As Sarah spent hours talking with women friends at work, she found she was growing increasingly confused. They were open to all kinds of options of family life for the future, of throwing out what had been considered the traditional normal family, and yet she did not think they were happy and fulfilled despite all their experimentations in different relationships and different lifestyles.

Toffler summed up what one or two of them expressed less well:

The Third Wave civilization will not try to stuff everyone willy-nilly into a single family form . . . this . . . could free us to find his or her own niche . . . but before anyone can perform a celebratory dance, the agonies of transition must be dealt with . . . millions find the higher level of diversity bewildering rather than helpful. Instead of suffering from liberation they suffer from overchoice and are wounded, embittered, plunged into a sorrow and loneliness intensified by the very multiplicity of their options.

To make this new diversity work for us instead of against us, we will need to make changes on many levels at once, from morality, to taxes, to employment practices.

In the field of values we need to begin by removing the unwanted guilt that accompanies the break-up and restructuring of families. Instead of exacerbating unjustified guilt, the media, the Church, the courts and the political system should be working to lower the guilt level.[8]

Sarah found that increasingly she was being swept up into the thinking of her colleagues at work. It was new, it was exciting, it was great to think that life could be filled with freshness, excitement, and brilliant and inspired insights into different ways of living – ways that got you out of the rut into which life had sunk for so many people in the postwar era. She was glad for Pete and for his openness to allowing her to be all that she felt she was created to be. What the Church thought about the issues she was facing, she had no idea. As far as she understood it, her church didn't think about issues like that and so there was no conflict. She could continue going to church and being her Sunday-type Sarah on the Sabbath, and the rest of the week be the career-woman Sarah whose ideas would have made little sense had she ever tried to express them to the church young wives group – which she didn't attend anyway as she was working by day and recovering from work every evening. Whether her wider thinking in recent years would be agreed to or contradicted by them she did not know – nor did she think to question, for it seemed strangely irrelevant to anything that she thought the Church or the Bible would be about.

In her heart of hearts, some questions were being thrown up which she desperately longed to have answered by a Christian – but no Christians seemed to be asking, let alone answering, questions like hers.

Ann Dally, a psychiatrist, put some of Sarah's thoughts on to paper with the words:

The young mother today, like the nineteenth-century bride, has little means of knowing what she is really in for. But, added to this, she has all the new problems of our time. Most people in the last century had no doubt

65

that family life was best, or that raising children was a duty to God. Now we are not so sure about the family, the children or God. We are uncertain about what kind of world we are raising our children into, and about how best to prepare them for it. Do we, for instance, deliberately prepare them for uncertainty and change? Or try to ignore the outside uncertainty and provide security within the family? Do we ignore the question altogether and bring them up according to how we feel or according to some abstract theory about what is "best" for children?

Our ancestors did not have to decide these questions . . . Motherhood has become full of uncertainty and paradox, fraught with dilemmas at all stages, arousing passion and anxiety, creating illusion and also being altered by it. It has thus become particularly liable to disillusion which is often catastrophic.[9]

As far as Sarah could see, she was almost the odd one out, in being married and in intending to stay married to Pete. Somewhere from childhood lingered the deep sense that marriage and family life as her parents had known it was something that was right and good . . . but she was not sure why! Her gut-level feeling that there was something basically good was echoed in puzzlement by Ferdinand Mount in his controversial book *The Subversive Family*:

The dominant force in the Western World is for the urban working class to fulfil its own aspirations. And among the first of those aspirations, most intimate and most ancient, is the desire for privacy, for equality and for independence *in marriage*.

Why [he asks] is it that this desire for the independence of marriage should continue to look stronger than the desire for personal independence, which is often said to be the dominant trend of our times?

Why [he persists in puzzling] do people still wish to submerge, at least partly, their personalities in marriage and devote a great part of their lives – perhaps a major part – to "working" at this battered old form of human relationship?

And, in the end, the answer he gives himself failed to satisfy Sarah:

[It] may be because marriage still seems to be the most interesting enterprise which most of us come across . . .[10]

"Shucks!" Sarah put the book to one side. "There's got to be more to it than that!" And she, like many others of her age and stage, began to seek a more satisfying answer as to why marriage is something so basic within human beings that it is given priority with little thought as to why this should be so.

Sarah realized that in Pete she had a man who, although a Christian, was willing for her to travel unhampered far further along the road traversed by the feminist movement than the average Christian husband. Yet there was still something missing in her marriage. She was fulfilled in her job. Her arms weren't aching for a baby. She wasn't broody – at least not yet! Had she found in her liberated marriage to a man who gave her freedom to do her own thing in her own way, that which God intended her marriage to be?

She'd never asked herself questions like that before. Asking them posed deeper questions and before long she found herself exploring the Bible in a way she would not have thought of before, had she not longed to discover whether her marriage was as complete as it was ever going to be, or whether it was possible that she and Pete were missing out on something that God intended for them.

Chapter 6

Angela turned to me from her highly organized freezer. I looked behind her to the shelves, stocked with carefully planned meals for her family for the next couple of weeks, and wished that I could be more efficient in my role as career-woman and homemaker, and more like her.

She was someone I admired tremendously. Not only did she run a home with clockwork smoothness but she had time for her husband and children and also held down a responsible job as the head of a department in a large secondary school. She held good degrees from Cambridge, and in her "spare" time she was mastering the intricacies of mathematics on a home computer. But above all, watching her and knowing how gifted she was, I coveted her ability to turn to her husband and to allow him to be the "head" of their home and family. I had seen her with her husband and knew her words were matched by practice.

She stood in sharp contrast to many Christian wives who have come to me in perplexity and even bitterness, complaining: "My husband won't be head of our family. He likes to think he is, but when it comes to the crunch, I'm left to run things and work out what seems best. Then I have to carry it through on my own. I long for him to be the man I believe he should be both to me and to our children . . ."

Many such complaints are justified, for we are now experiencing some of the results of the assumptions and teachings of current culture that unisex attitudes should be assimilated into everyday life and be allowed to infiltrate everything – even marriage. Popular magazines hint at this in their writings about the demise of the so-called "macho man" and the advent of the "wimp".

A new generation of Christian husbands includes men who are trying to do their best for their wives and to pick out that which is good in current culture and act on it. They have rightly realized that part of good husbanding is to allow their wives to develop their full potential – and that part is great! However, some do this at the expense of failing to exercise their God-given role of being the "head" of their wives. When asked why they do this, the reply is an embarrassed confession that amounts to the fact that they do not know what headship is, or how it could possibly apply to them in their particular relationship with their wives.

Headship to them appears to be an authoritarian dictatorship – something that has been discarded along with a lot of Victorian ideals and is best relegated to the trunk in the attic labelled "remnants from when great-grandma was alive . . . for Memory Lane only".

Marriage is seen as a partnership, as companionship combined with love and the right assumption that "each of us is as good as the other".

But Sally expressed her feeling about what was happening to her in her marriage with the words: "There's something that makes me feel incomplete . . . not quite satisfied that my marriage is what it should be. But I don't know what is missing."

What is happening in some Christian marriages today? Why do some feel that their relationship is incomplete and not totally fulfilled? John Stott writes about this clearly:

Of course, men need women ("it is not good for man to be alone"), but women also need men! Masculine headship is intended not to suppress but to serve them, and to ensure that they are – and may more fully become – themselves . . .

The resolute desire of women to know, be and even develop themselves, and to use their gifts in the service of the world, is so obviously God's will for them, that to deny or frustrate it is an extremely serious oppression. It is a woman's basic right and responsibility to discover herself, her identity and vocation. The fundamental question is, in what relationship with men will women find and be themselves?

Certainly not in subordination which implies inferiority to men and engenders low self-esteem . . . Equality and partnership between the sexes are sound biblical concepts. But not if they are pressed into denying a masculine headship of protective care. It is surely a distorted headship of domination which has convinced women that they cannot find themselves in this way.

Only the biblical ideal of headship, which because it is selflessly loving may justly be called "Christ-like", can convince them it will facilitate, and not destroy their true identity.[1]

But some women will shrink from the words "masculine headship of protective care"! What does John Stott mean? Is he saying that today's Christian woman needs wrapping in cotton wool to stop her from being broken by the culture in which we live? As she leaves home for her day's work as MP, long-distance lorry driver, farmer, chairperson of multinational companies, brain surgeon and so on, does she really want men to treat her with "protective care"? Unlikely! If these words are taken at face value, then she is likely to run a million miles from anyone who would try to cocoon her from life and its harsh realities – for she knows intuitively that in some ways she is even better equipped to face life than many of her male counterparts!

Some men who marry today's modern women neither want, nor dare, to think in terms of "protecting" their partners. They may even feel that the situation should be reversed and that their all-competent wives should protect them! The wife who is omnicompetent, abounding in energy, sustaining and protecting, may, in fact, assume a role that is more that of mother than marriage partner. The man may give up with little struggle and be submerged in her gifts and abilities, allowing her free rein to be what she wants to be and to do what she want to do.

Is it wrong then for men to try to allow their partners to develop to their maximum potential? Surely not! The emphasis in the last twenty years or so in Christian marriage has been the rightful rediscovery of ancient biblical concepts.

As Angela expressed it, something good had happened to her: "Jim and I feel we understand what the Bible is talking about when it refers to marriage as a relationship of companionship. We really are best friends with one another. We delight in the fact that we can relate as equals. And more than that we are blessed in that we can spar mentally — there's a sort of intellectual stimulation as our minds sharpen one another's thinking. I've found that because Jim understands me so well, things from my childhood that have hurt me for years have been brought to the surface, and he's been able to help to heal old wounds that I thought I'd have to live with for the rest of my life. It's a joy to work together on the house, in the garden, and to bring up our children together. It's often difficult for us to remember that he's male and I am female . . ."

Yet, looking at Jim and Angela together it's obvious from the way he treats her that the differences between them as man and woman are there, and that each recognizes these in practicalities. "I do want to care for Angela and the children properly," Jim says shyly.

In their partnership of equality they have learned that for a woman to be successful, she does not necessarily have to be the one of the couple who exerts the power in the home. And, in a power-centred culture, they have learned an important lesson for marriage.

Turn on the TV set and watch the advertisements for a

few minutes and you soon see what our culture thinks of power in the hands of women. One type of "ideal" woman strides aggressively, drink in hand (metaphorically if not physically), over some poor, dejected male who is not using the paint she has chosen for guaranteed success, fails to wield the power derived from a certain brand of petrol, or is incapable of cutting the lawn as effectively as she – wonder woman – can do with a certain brand of mower!

Our world sees the powerful person as someone who is valuable and important. The powerful woman, in the implied message of some advertisements and magazine articles, is the one who will be a success – married or otherwise is irrelevant! Current culture, with its admiration for power, is communicating values that are the opposite of those in the New Testament. Jesus said: "Blessed are the meek, for they will inherit the earth" (Matthew 5:5).

The Apostle Paul wrote: "But (God) said to me, 'My grace is sufficient for you, for my power is made perfect in weakness.' Therefore, I will boast all the more gladly about my weaknesses, so that Christ's power may rest on me" (2 Corinthians 12:10). It was written of Jesus: "He is able to deal gently with those who are ignorant and are going astray, since he himself is subject to weakness" (Hebrews 5:2).

Those Christian women who write, it seems incessantly, to Christian magazines with their cry: "Why are Christian men so wet?" have a point to make, yet behind their cry can be heard the more subtle complaint that there is something wrong with someone who is not strong or who is powerless.

Biblical teaching indicates that weakness is not something to be despised, and that power is not something to be prized. Christians are encouraged to be different from the pressures to conform to today's world, with words like these: "Your attitude should be the same as that of Christ Jesus: Who, being in very nature God, did not consider equality with God something to be grasped, but made himself nothing, taking the very nature of a servant, being made in human likeness . . . He humbled himself and became obedient to death – even death on a cross! Therefore, God exalted him to the highest place . . ." (Philippians 2:6–8).

Our culture has taught us to despise weakness, but this is not the teaching of the Bible. Therefore, it is natural for today's Christian woman to shrink from words like: "Husbands . . . be considerate as you live with your wives, and treat them with respect as the weaker partner . . ." (1 Peter 3:7).

Some will react with the words: "Rubbish . . . the Apostle Peter obviously doesn't know what he's talking about!" And some husbands too may shrink for another reason, thinking: "I can't do that . . . my wife's the strong one of the two of us!" Truth lies behind both these reactions! So, what then is the Bible seeking to communicate?

I believe that John Stott comes to the heart of the matter when he says:

> Under the rubric of "weakness" we should probably include those characteristically female traits of gentleness, tenderness, sensitivity, patience and devotion. These are delicate plants, which are easily trodden underfoot, and which wither and die if the climate is unfriendly. I cannot see that it is demeaning to a woman to say that masculine "headship" is the God-given means by which their femininity is protected and enabled to blossom.[2]

A picture is emerging from the Bible of a "head" who is not an authoritative dictator, but rather who is a servant and who leads by selfless giving and cherishing of his wife. This is the way in which the Lord Jesus loved the Church – and husbands are commanded to love their wives in exactly this manner.

The husband is the head of the wife as Christ is the head of the Church, his body, of which he is the Saviour . . . Husbands, love your wives, just as Christ loved the Church and gave himself up for her to make her holy, cleansing her by the washing with water through the word, and to present her to himself as a radiant Church, without stain or wrinkle or any other blemish, but holy and blameless. In this way, husbands ought to love their wives as their own bodies. He who loves his wife loves himself. After all, no one ever hated his own body, but he feeds it and cares for it, just as Christ does the Church . . . (Ephesians 5:23–29).

The people to whom this epistle was written did not have our modern understanding of how the body's central nervous system functions, nor of the exact role which the brain plays in controlling the body's actions. Their understanding of the head in relation to the rest of the body was that the head was the part of the body which integrated and nurtured the rest. To them, Paul's words about headship would have referred more to care than to control, and to responsibility rather than to authority. John Stott explains:

As her head [the husband] gives himself up for her in love, just as Christ did for his body the Church. And he looks after her, as we do our own bodies. His concern is not to crush her, but to liberate her. As Christ gave himself for his bride, in order to present her to himself radiant and blameless, so the husband gives himself for his bride in order to create the conditions in which she may grow into the fullness of her femininity.[3]

Under the supportive care of her husband, John Stott believes that a woman is able to flower more fully in her femininity. I agree with him!

So to some extent do two other Christian women writers. "The father's role," says Elizabeth Catherwood, "biblically is clearly vital; he is the final authority, the lover, the cherisher of the mother, the wisely disciplining, non-provoking, caring, compassionate head of his little family."[4]

The same idea is expressed by Valerie Griffiths: "To encourage some people to exert their masculinity by cutting across other people's wishes is scarcely Christian, and is a recipe for disaster. However, where the wife respects her husband, where the husband honours his wife, where each in humility counts the other better than themselves, there is a basis for respect, mutual consultation, love and unity."[5]

This is why problems arise in a marriage when a husband fails to exercise his God-given headship – no matter what the reason for this may be. The result is likely to be that his wife is not as fully feminine as she could be if he was cherishing and supporting her as God intended. And his family life fails to blossom and flourish as God meant it to.

Life today has yet other pressures which discourage men from being the full men which God created them to be. David Field explains:

The erosion of personal responsibility . . . we live in times when it is more fashionable to shelve responsibility than to take it. Inasmuch as accepting authority implies accepting responsibility, there are many husbands who are only too willing for their wives to make all the choices and take all the decisions.

Life is nearly always easier that way – assuming, of course, that they (the husbands) are free to "do their own thing" in the meantime . . . For every married man who has been pushed off the domestic throne against his will there are three or four others who have simply and gladly abdicated."[6]

The frustration expressed to me by some Christian wives bears out the truth of David Field's words. Some summed it up to me in words like: "He's got it cushy . . .he does what he wants to and leaves me to run everything, and make sure that everything works out . . . I don't think that's either fair or right!"

"If a wife loses her submission to her husband, she loses her unity with him. If a husband abdicates his responsibility as head, he strikes at the very core of the relationship which God has established between him and his wife . . ." says Larry Christenson.[7] At first glance it may appear that he cannot be right. Yet careful thought shows that what he says is based on biblical truth.

In biblical language, the "two have become one flesh" in marriage. Therefore, the husband who abuses his headship is ultimately hurting not only his wife but also himself. The man who abdicates his headship and does not carry his God-given responsibility may, in this way, harm himself. While the Bible is clear that in principle the husband is to be head of his wife, precisely how this is to be worked out in practice is not spelled out. If the husband accepts that one of his headship responsibilities involves him in seeing that his wife has the freedom she needs to grow as a person and to develop her potential fully, then this will find different ways of expression.

For a minority this might just involve the man running the home, and the wife being the main breadwinner outside the home. Does this differ from the basic teachings of the feminist movement? David Field answers:

By and large, feminism works by competition and confrontation, and takes its stand on a wife's right to make independent choices. The principle of headship, by contrast, is more concerned to foster unity and mutual growth, and leaves the ultimate decision-making to the husband.[8]

This is just one of the many ways in which Christians who are married today need to distinguish between what is biblical and what is cultural, and thus avoid the confusion facing many couples. Honesty and an unflinching desire for integrity must undergird every examination of motives, assumptions and reasons as to why certain things are done in certain ways. Then God's truth can be discerned. For instance, the woman working outside her home might need to ask herself whether she is doing this and finding fulfilment in it under the headship of a husband who has encouraged her in it, or whether she has grabbed any chances that have come her way and barely given her husband the opportunity to say what he thinks – let alone to express his deeper feelings. The fact that she has apparently run over him like a steamroller (and possibly not even noticed she has done just this) may leave him feeling very diminished as a man.

On the other hand, the man who expresses lavish praise for the wife who seems able to do nearly everything (and does it) may have opted for a cushy life against her wishes and actually abdicated his responsibility and headship role. He may have left her to handle all the difficult matters because he can't be bothered to take them up himself. Is he lazy, incompetent, or psychologically unable to carry responsibility?

What about the young wife, left alone all day at home with tiny children and driven to distraction and boredom by lack of intellectual stimulation and no adult company? Has her husband ever stopped to ask himself what his caring nourishment of her could and should be? Are there ways in which he could sacrifice himself to allow her time and space away from the children, to develop more fully as a person and to learn how to mature as the woman God intends her to be? Unless you have been cooped up with small children for a long time and sunk from demoralization into the depths of clinical depression, then it may be difficult for you to understand what effect this lifestyle can have on some women. Is the husband of such a woman doing all he can to help lift her load, share it, or is he seeking his own comfort before anything else?

On the other hand, some wives may feel that they have been "put out to work" when really they long for nothing more than to be allowed to stay at home and to mother their children. They may long to live on less money – but their husbands may not have even considered this as a viable option.

No two Christian marriages will ever be the same. Within the rich and glorious diversity of the way in which God has created each person as a unique individual, each two different people combine to make a unique marriage. God's amazing patterns are smashed where couples feel they must conform to what appears to be the norm, rather than face being slightly different in their particular lifestyle and thus possibly face gossip, criticism and the whispered, "Their marriage is quite odd – it doesn't seem to be really biblical . . ." When this happens, God's rich variety in marriage is diminished. God does not intend marriage to be grey conformity.

Understandably, today's emphasis on the feminist movement and its awareness of the roles and rights of women, has brought a decreased emphasis on the place and the importance of men. Some have felt devalued by our culture and of less value in the family than their fathers were. Some have felt incompetent and scared by the new race of "superwomen", who are not only intensely practical and can do all the things men used to do (plumbing, decorating and electrical wiring), but also seem overwhelmingly clever intellectually. Few men like to admit this!

Some heave a sigh of relief and hide behind the TV set or their newspaper, leaving all responsibility to their wives . . . never questioning whether this course of evasive action is best for them, for their wives or for their children. What, for instance, are their children learning about responsible husbanding and fatherhood?

Other men have been flattened by wives who are keen to express themselves, to be themselves, and who have not noticed the crushed remnants of their husbands left to wilt in an armchair. Yet others have meekly lain down on the doormats of their first homes and allowed their brides to walk right over them time and time again! Little have they suspected that the new wife was simply trying out an old role of school prefect, just to assert herself and never intending to set a pattern that would last a lifetime.

Unless men start being men and assuming the masculine role that God has given to them, and unless they function as caring, nourishing, responsible heads of their wives and families, then the next generation will have inadequate models on which to base their husbanding and parenting in the future. If this happens then the next generation of Christian marriages could become far too "female dominated" and exhibit far too few of the qualities that God commands and demands, that come when men are truly men.

Christian men must again be masculine and women feminine – and the lessons of headship and submission must be learned and practised in a truly biblical manner. If this is done, then barriers will be erected that will help Christian marriages to stand against the attacks currently being made to destroy them.

If Christian husbands and wives learn these lessons, then Christian families are less likely to become part of the statistics of the one in seven families currently headed by a single parent. Families will stay together because the marriage is welded on timeless God-given principles that are designed to stand the strain that culture can place on them.

Chapter 7

Like colliding billiard balls, Mary and Steve bumped into one another, fell in love, and within a few days of their first meeting sensed that God had thrown them together and that they were to remain close for life. Both were thrown off the tracks they had previously assumed their lives would follow. And, being "in love", their lives assumed an intangible ecstatic quality which made it impossible for them to view the future as dispassionately or objectively as others often wanted them to.

Friends and relatives joked about the rose-coloured spectacles the couple now wore, but beneath those jokes lay an unuttered wistfulness – almost envy – for the beautiful, fragile and precious discovery the couple had made. It was something magnetic that drew them powerfully and almost irresistibly to one another. It was greater than pure sexual desire and yet it was very different from friendship.

In being together, each discovered his or her identity in a different dimension from that which they had recognized in themselves in the past. Through love – loving and being loved – each found within their inner selves untapped resources of potential that they had failed to uncover before. Through one another, they unlocked one of the mysteries of love – that love holds within it the power to bring to the surface what is best and truest in the other: that which is concealed and often buried deep within the personality.

For a woman, an intimate sexual encounter based on deep love draws out an expression of herself in its most revealing and profound manner. And this mystery of "knowing and being known" is tied up with one of the mysteries of marriage – that referred to in biblical terms as the "one fleshness" of a couple which lives together within the framework of a committed, exclusive sexual union. The Bible says: "For this reason a man will leave his father and mother and be united to his wife, and they will become one flesh . . ." (Genesis 2:24).

The meaning of the words "one flesh union" can be taken simply at face value to mean that through sexual intercourse two people join as one, but the words also contain deeper significance. This is explained by A. C. Thiselton:

> The union of man and woman creates a new relationship. "One flesh" does not in the first instance mean sexual intercourse, though it includes it. It signifies the coming into being of a unitary existence, a complete partnership of man and woman which cannot be broken up without damage to the partners in it. This does not mean that every marriage is automatically such a complete partnership. Rather, this complete partnership is the promise of marriage which should be claimed. It is the meaning of marriage granted by God.[1]

As Jesus stated: "So they are no longer two, but one. Therefore what God has joined together, let man not separate" (Matthew 19:6).

Comprehending some of the meanings of the word that is translated in the Bible as "flesh" helps us understand what is being communicated to us. The Hebrew word has several different meanings, including, as A. C. Thiselton writes, that of a human being himself:

> The self does not stand alone, however. A relative is "bone of my bone and flesh of my flesh" "Then Laban said to him, 'You are my own flesh and blood'" (Genesis 29:14). Accordingly, "The man said, 'This is now bone of my bones and flesh of my flesh; she shall be called "woman" for she was taken out of man'" (Genesis 2:23).

Genesis 2:23 means: woman is for man, as it were, the place in the world where he is at home. Her intimate relationship creates his home.[2]

But how does this take place? The explanation cannot be scientific, it has to be theological. Gerhard von Rad suggests:

> A fact needs explanation, namely, the extremely powerful drive of the sexes to each other. Whence comes this "love strong as death" (Song of Solomon 8:6) and stronger than the tie to one's own parents, whence this inner clinging to each other, this drive towards each other . . . it comes from the fact that God took woman from man, and they actually were originally one flesh. Therefore, they must come together again and thus by destiny they belong to each other.[3]

This does not imply that we are half people, never resting till we find the other half of ourselves. Rather, that man without woman is incomplete and vice versa. There is not one perfectly matching partner designed for each human being who must be found at all costs.

Derek Kidner explains:

> [Man] will not live until he loves, giving himself away to another on his own level. So the woman is presented wholly as his partner and counterpart; nothing is yet said of her as childbearer. She is valued for herself alone . . . the union of the two in marriage is to be an exclusive, permanent, God-sealed bond; for God himself like the father of a bride, leads the woman to the man . . .
>
> There is, in God's true pattern, perfect ease between them . . . but it is the fruit of perfect love which has no alloy of greed, distrust or dishonour; it was

understandably an immediate casualty of the Fall . . .
(Genesis 2:18).

Man's new consciousness of good and evil was both
like and unlike the divine knowledge, differing from it
and from innocence as a sick man's aching awareness of
his body differs both from the insights of the physician
and the unconcern of the man in health . . . The couple
now ill at ease together, experienced a foretaste of fallen
human relations in general.[4]

This meeting and joining together of a man and a woman
was what God designed as the best way in which each could
live a fulfilled life. John Burnaby says:

When Adam was created, the Lord God said: "It is not
good for the man to be alone: I will make a helpmeet for
him" (Genesis 2:18). Man is a social animal, and the love of
man and woman, of parents and children, links his nature
to the life of bird and beast. But the things that put man
above the animals, the developments of language, thought
and culture, have not altered and never can alter men's
ultimate need of one another – not for the supply of any
other needs, but to make their very humanity human.

Self-sufficiency is the negation of humanity. We can
only be persons in virtue of the personal relationships
which unite us to one another in mutual exchange. Our
life can only be lived to the full by being shared with
others – and not with others in general but with certain
others in particular . . .

And love cannot fulfil itself in a one-way process:
unless there is both giving and receiving, love must
remain unsatisfied . . . the measure of true love is just its
power to feel its way into the consciousness of the other:
to love our neighbour as ourself, if we could ever do it,
would be to realize his existence and his needs as vividly
as if they were our own.

What we call sympathy is really essential to love; and sympathy, though it requires imagination, the ability to picture in one's own mind what is passing in the mind of another, is always more than imagination: it is the actual sharing of experience . . . their joy and their sorrow are genuinely felt and experienced as our own.[5]

Because marriage and sexual union as designed by God holds within it an unfathomable and sacred meaning, it is all the more tragic that with the Fall of man (through disobedience in the Garden of Eden) has come contamination and a devaluation of this unique gift given to mankind to complete and fulfil him as a person. History reveals, as does modern culture, the sad results in civilizations that have discarded the sanctity of marriage and exchanged it for promiscuous sexual relationships. The results? Men and women whose capacity to relate to others in meaningful and healing ways has been impaired by the emotional scars of casual sexual intercourse – based often on little more than lust, loneliness or boredom. And those scars remain in many people, impairing eventual marriage relationships so that they are less rewarding than they would have been had sexual intercourse not been used as a means to an end – an instant gratification of immediate needs. According to God's plan, sexual union was intended to express the communion and commitment that can be given to one person only – one's chosen life partner.

For Steve and Mary, marriage provided the framework in which their mutual love could be expressed and each could give to the other and find fulfilment and satisfaction at the deepest levels of their personalities. "I never knew what I was missing till I married Mary!" Steve confided. "I feel whole . . . although I never knew I was incomplete till I became one with her . . ."

But Mary found an even deeper enrichment through being Steve's wife. The losing of her maiden name and her maidenhead (she was a virgin when she married) was the first time that she had given herself totally to another person. She identified with Thielicke's words:

> The wife gives her "self" when she gives herself sexually. She holds nothing back and precisely in doing this she comes to her self-realization . . . man is not nearly so deeply stamped and moulded by his sexual experience as is the case with the woman . . . Out of the centre of her nature the woman strives to make the totality of her experience correspond with her total submission to the man. Her goal is to make not only the physical side of the man her own, not merely once or temporarily, but rather to own the man's very self . . . Feminine sexuality . . . lies in the urge towards self-realization . . . In her incapability of separating the physical from the personal ignoring the "person" of the man would promote loss of self-hood rather than effect sought-after realization.[6]

The differences in God's design of men and women do much to enhance the enrichment of the experience of two such different beings becoming "one flesh". Not only are they different in gender, but each also brings to the marriage the differences they represent in personality types. And these differences hold within them the greatest potential possible, both for increased understanding of life and of other people, and also great potential for misunderstanding and alienation from the very one who is intended to bring harmony and increased integration.

Mary and Steve barely noticed the differences between their characters when they fell in love and married. It was only years later that Steve was able to look back and reflect: "She and I are totally different but complementary people. We come to better decisions when we talk things through together than we could as individuals – we blend together my male logical approach to problems plus her intuitive sense of what would or wouldn't work." But I know that for him to reach this point of accepting their differences as a bonus, rather than as a threat to his masculinity, has taken years of developing a relationship of mutual understanding.

The "one flesh union" of a couple may be deeply satisfying sexually, but God intends it to go far deeper and way beyond that alone. However, such a deep relationship is achieved only after hard work and deliberate effort at understanding one's partner, and displaying a willingness to open oneself up to one's partner. The anthropologist Jacob Loewens rightly states: "Self-revelation is the bridge to understanding." Until partners learn to give themselves, thus making themselves vulnerable to rejection and misunderstanding, they will not learn fully to receive from one another. The bridge of revelation stretching between the two must be mutual and not a one-sided sharing of the deep things that matter by one partner and silence from the other.

Many middle-aged couples, who have never grasped this point, find themselves like Ann and Henry. They live together under the same roof, share the same bank account, experience physical intimacy a couple of times a month, but have never really opened themselves up to one another. Ann says: "We've never really argued about anything. Henry's never said anything unkind or hurtful to me. We pass the time of day with each other. But apart from that, there's nothing much between us."

Henry comments: "We've got used to being with one another and so we'll stay together – but there's nothing really deep to bind us together beyond the comfort of familiarity."

"Now the children have left," Ann adds, "I can see that what appeared to be our wonderful family life was built on a shell of a relationship between Henry and me. And we never realized it was possible to experience anything different till I started reading recently and saw that in marriage a relationship could be different."

Some men, like Henry, actually prefer to try to live independent, self-sufficient lives. They genuinely do not want the bother of getting involved with their wives at any deep level. It is easy to escape, pleading heavy work responsibilities, disappearing behind the newspaper, falling asleep in front of the television, and when the wife finally does attract enough attention to have to be listened to, to adopt a tone of vague disinterest that makes her feel that what she wants to discuss is, after all, of too little significance to be taken seriously. Or he can simply pass it off with the words: "What's the fuss? You're het up again. Must be the time of the month . . ."

Other men (and women) are afraid of developing any deep relationships and therefore the easy way out is to avoid opportunities for encountering another person at any level that is profound enough to pose a threat. But not only is the building of a deep relationship part of God's intention in a "one flesh" marriage relationship, it is also necessary to the development of men and women as mature personalities. And such a relationship does not appear on the first day of the honeymoon, it takes time – often years – of building trust so that each feels safe enough with the other to reveal both the good and the bad, in the knowledge that such revelation is respected, accepted non-judgementally and lovingly.

A deep encounter often comes only after hours of careful work, so that when sudden sharing at a deep level is needed, a situation of trust already exists in which it is natural and easy to share. Most of us need to muster up courage before we dare to reveal our inner thoughts to another. But until we unveil our inner selves to our partners, understanding cannot begin to grow. And revealing to our partners those things about which we are most ashamed is both the hardest and yet, paradoxically, the most rewarding thing that we can do in our quest for a richer and more God-reflecting marriage.

If you are quick to criticize your partner then you inflict on him or her far deeper hurts than another person would – for you are the one closest to him and from whom he most needs loving support and acceptance. "I've no idea why my wife's like that . . ." can be words that leave a wife feeling judged, condemned and criticized, without even stating her case. She knows full well that there is plenty wrong with her, without her husband's added blame, and often she is not pleased with herself either! His unspoken verdict, "failure", does no more than make her even less self-accepting and feel even more of a failure than she was before.

Criticism from a partner can cause needless hurt and smoulder into resentment. Gratuitous advice given when not requested can hurt just as much as direct criticism, for it says implicitly: "You aren't doing very well. I know better than you. Do it my way."

The partner who wants to share something needs a situation in which he or she knows he will be listened to with love and sympathy. Critical faculties need not be suspended, but the partner needs to be assured that he is loved and accepted for himself, regardless of anything he may or may not have done. And as we learn to understand the other, we need to learn to listen, and listen and listen. Moral judgements of "that was wrong" or "that was good" are out of place in this special kind of listening designed to draw two people close across a bridge of understanding. In such situations, the one who is sharing, often through the very experience of sharing, begins to see things in a light different from his former perspective and, as a direct result, may even change the shape of his thinking and actions.

Someone who is understood in this way feels loved and at one with the person with whom he shares. Out of this oneness springs the natural expression of total unity – the total giving of self – which for women is best expressed through sexual intercourse. Paradoxically, it is out of loving that understanding develops and vice versa. The two go hand in hand.

While women find it relatively easy to share deep emotional feelings with someone they trust, it is hard for most men. Men tend to hide their secrets, hugging them tightly to themselves, feeling sure that they could never be shared with another person. Yet, within the context of an accepting, non-judgemental, understanding and loving relationship some men who appear to be "closed books" sometimes reveal things they thought could never be shared with another human being. This is another aspect of "one fleshness".

On the partner receiving such confidences lies the responsibility of receiving them in such a way that the importance of what is being shared is not minimized or trivialized, not despised or laughed at, not glossed over and barely even heard, and that the pain involved in the telling does not go uneased through the way in which it is received.

Those who share and whose words are not really heard with loving understanding may be left feeling desperate. "I told her how black life was since my mother died", Pete shared. "She just said I ought to snap out of it, and would I go and change the baby's nappy . . . and I knew I couldn't ever try and share anything important with her again. She didn't care about my pain. I needed her arms around me to make things right . . . I didn't need words – just her love."

Paul Tournier comments:

It is not good that man should be alone. Man here means the human being: "It is not good that the human being should be alone." The human being needs fellowship, he needs a partner, a real encounter with others. He needs to understand others, and to sense that others understand him. Such is the very institution of God in instituting marriage – according to the Bible. Alone, a man marks time and becomes very set in his ways. In the demanding confrontation which marriage constitutes, he must ever go beyond himself, develop and grow up into maturity. When marriage is reduced to mere symbiosis of two people essentially hidden from one another, peaceful though such a life may sometimes be, it has completely missed its goal. Then it is not solely the marriage that has failed but the husband and the wife. They have failed in their calling as man and woman. To fail to understand one's spouse is to fail to understand oneself. It is also a failure to grow and to fulfil one's possibilities.[7]

Tournier identifies three distinct phases through which most couples pass, either in their development towards a richer "one flesh union" or in growing apart from one another.

First of all, many, like Mary and Steve, find during the early years of marriage that there is an almost uncanny and intuitive sense of mutual understanding and completeness. They know what the other is going to say, and can finish off sentences mid-air for the other. They know how their partner will feel and react to given situations. This sense of intuitive awareness of the other binds them together. Many people choose a partner who is totally different from themselves – someone who complements them and compensates for their weak points. Thus, the joining together of such opposites can lead to a sense of completeness. What is lacking in me, is present in the one to whom I am now joined. I feel whole and marvellous!

After five to ten years, this feeling of completeness is blunted by the objectivity of realizing that one's partner is actually not quite as similar to oneself as first appeared. The faults that were not noticed have surfaced, and the faults you hoped you could cure by waving the magic wand of marriage over them are still there and may even be magnified – if not to others, at least to you.

What happens next depends on the handling of this stage in marriage. If progressively you give up what seems to be a fruitless and worthless struggle for happiness and give in to resentment, bitterness and rebellion, then you may find that life becomes a round of endless arguments that are never settled – and divorce seems the only way out of an unhappy coupling of two who can no longer relate. On the other hand, each may give up his or her personality and stop struggling to be his or her own person simply for a peaceful life. Agreement may be reached to live within marriage at a much lower level of communication and understanding than was originally desired.

Alternatively, the best way of handling your relationship when this stage is reached is to see your partner as he or she really is – without those rose-coloured spectacles that have for so long prevented you from seeing, understanding and accepting reality along with romantic love. This means really getting to know the partner who now seems so unattractive to you, who is laden with hang-ups, peculiar ideas and idiosyncrasies. If you can begin truly to love despite all this – and love not only for good points but just as much for weaknesses and problems, then you can rebuild your marriage on a lasting foundation.

"Those who make a success of their marriages are those who tackle their problems together and who overcome them," says Paul Tournier. "Those who lack the courage to do this are the ones whose marriage is a failure."[8]

Tackling these problems requires some insights as to the basic differences between men and women. Although there are few men who will ever really understand a woman, and vice versa! Men tend to think in terms of theories and principles, while women will orientate their thinking around people.

"What moral guidelines are there in this to help us sort out the situation we are facing?" a man may ask his wife. Her reply may surprise him if it is: "Do make sure that So-and-So isn't hurt by what you're planning to do, as she's the most vulnerable person in this situation." He asked about guidelines, but she thought of people!

A man's actions may seem cruel to a woman. He may be struggling to establish righteousness and has not noticed the secretary in the corner of the room who has been hurt. His wife sees the secretary and wishes he had gone about his crusade with greater sensitivity to the individual caught in the scenario. Women bring into society a sensitivity for people, and without them society would be technical, cold and dehumanized. Another major difference between the sexes is that women tend to think of details, while men look at broad vistas – to them the details are insignificant.

Women tend to be able to express their emotions in words, while men are often dumb on such matters. The opposite occurs in *Fiddler on the Roof* where the old man asks his wife: "Do you love me?" She replies: "For forty years I've mended your shoes, cleaned your house, cooked your food, slept in your bed . . . how can you ask, do I love you?" Speech for men is the means of expressing ideas and passing on information. For women it is the means of releasing pent-up tension, expressing deep feelings, and getting things out of the system.

Ann explained: "Every night when he came home from work he'd give me a diary-like account of what he'd done that day. He never told me what he thought or felt . . . just passed on all this information, but I wasn't desperately interested in it. I wanted to know about the people in his office, what they thought and said, but he never seemed to know or else forgot to tell me that kind of thing."

"She goes on and on about the same things . . . " Henry complained. "Once something's upset her she doesn't stop talking about it, till I get so fed up I want to gag her!"

To Ann, her husband's work was almost something that took him away from her and shut her out of understanding of his life. To Henry, work was the most important thing in his life. Ann lived for home and family, Henry for work. The failure of each to share and to listen attentively with understanding to the other led them in middle age to the discovery that their relationship was flimsy and precarious.

Couples may also differ from each other in other ways, as Paul Tournier explains:

The basic differences between human types: extroverts who love social life, gaiety and movement, and introverts who seek tranquillity and serious thought. C. G. Jung has described them and has also shown us that reason and sentiment are like opposite poles, as are intuition and realism. Instinctively a very rational man is going to marry a very sentimental woman. Their complementing one another will, at the beginning, elicit an enthusiastic reaction in him. But later on he will want to make her listen to the objective arguments of reason; he will become annoyed at not being successful in this. He will try and show her that she is not logical in her sentimental explosions. This does not worry her at all. On her part she will reproach her husband for his ice-cold rational manner which stifles all life.

In the same way a scientific mind and an intuitive mind will have great difficulty in understanding each other. For the latter things are not what they objectively seem, but rather values of other values which he imagines and associates with them. For the former things are precisely what they are, nothing can be but that which can be weighed and measured. People so very different by nature are nevertheless made to complement each other, that through each other they may discover so much of what they've not known or sensed before. This is one of the purposes of marriage.[9]

Contemporary society has told us that marriage today is about finding fulfilment and understanding in our partners. It's there in the magazines and TV programmes and emphasized in a way that my grandmother's generation would think was exaggerated.

Today, couples live longer and therefore could get to know one another far better than in the past – was it not for the fact that only two out of three marriages continue and do not end in the divorce courts. We are taught that we should "keep in touch with our feelings". We should know when we feel hurt, rejected, misunderstood and angry. More than that, we are told we ought to understand why we feel as we do! If we can do this, then, the argument goes, we will live more richly and with less bitterness.

Obviously it does help me to recognize that on certain days I am reacting as I am because I am feeling depressed. It helps me even more if I can understand some of the childhood losses that may trigger off depression on any one day, so that I can deliberately try to set my mind in another groove and not to play the old record of reacting to certain situations by being depressed.

It helps me even more if my husband can understand me as well as I understand myself. If he notices that I am depressed before I have picked up the warning signs myself, and has pinpointed possible reasons, then together we can take steps to prevent it from getting worse. To know that he understands and accepts me despite this side of me (which I would prefer not to have and dislike) is healing and sustaining.

But I have watched other couples and heard the husband laughingly say: "She's in one of her moods again!" I've cringed, knowing how his wife must feel. His tone of voice somehow suggests that it is her fault that she is depressed. She is to blame for being like that, and her husband doesn't like it (or her). Message delivered and received loud and clear! She feels rejected for that which she cannot help – hormonal changes in her body causing premenstrual tension. And, instead of the couple drawing close to try to handle life together at such times, they draw apart, the wife feeling rejected and guilty.

It is at this nitty-gritty level of understanding and accepting one another that "one fleshness" works out in practice. Unless this tough work of mutual understanding is carried out, many couples end up by turning their backs on one another with the words "incompatible" or "irreversible breakdown in our relationship". But that stage could have been prevented had the oneness of sexual union been allowed to be part of a oneness in understanding and being understood.

For many of us, sharing ourselves with our partners involves reliving childhood experiences and areas from our past that have contributed to making us the people we are now. Knowing this is vital to understanding each other. Something may occur in marriage, however, that may be confusing unless you know what is happening and why. Dr Jack Dominian says this about close intimacy:

[It] has profound psychological implications whose roots stem from the world of the psychoanalysts . . . when a therapist sees a patient many times a week then transference develops . . . in the intimacy of the therapeutic relationship, patients relive their childhood experiences and treat the therapist as a significant figure from their childhood . . . the patient relives childhood experiences of conflict, anger, love, sexual feelings, deprivation etc.

Transference . . . occurs whenever two people have a continuous and intimate relationship, and contemporary marriage is one such relationship . . . we relive our original conflicts, anger, need for love, sexual feelings, fear of rejection, insecurities etc. . . .

All marriages undergo this transference to a variable degree and the transference can have a major healing effect, as it plainly does in the majority of marriages. But unresolved emotional problems can overwhelm the couple.[10]

Understanding the mosaic of past experiences that has made your partner the person he or she is now, can be richly rewarding and healing for both of you – as long as you understand the mechanism of transference and handle it gently and sensitively should it occur. Don't allow transference to threaten you, make you feel guilty or insecure.

When such understanding occurs, Paul Tournier says:

> Each is able to go beyond the natural reflexes of his personality type and of his sex. There is complete exchange. Each gives to the other that which was most missing. It is no longer a question of masculine or feminine love, but much more deeply human love in which each particular aspect of love is integrated. Finally there is a sense of oneness which is not realized until they are sure that they no longer have anything hidden from each other.[11]

If all this seems beyond the bounds of possibility, it helps to remember that it is the Holy Spirit himself who can enable this to work out in our human relationships. Tournier says:

> The breath of God's Spirit . . . no other force in the world can touch a man more deeply in his heart and make him more apt, at last, at understanding others. He sees his responsibilities, he understands that he was hurting the person whom he did not understand. He realizes that failure to understand and unwillingness to seek understanding are what caused his withdrawal into blind self-centredness.[12]

If we have not reached that stage of understanding yet, all is not lost. Tournier goes on to say:

> We can ask God to lead us there. To show us the way, himself to bring the total unity which is, according to his plan, to be the experience of marriage.
>
> Whatever one's past experiences may have been, new clouds will always appear. Just as soo, then, as our sensitive feelings are hurt again, our first instinctive reaction will always be to clam up, to withdraw, and to hide our real self.

And then, speaking of his own marriage, he says:

> But in our silent moments in God's presence, silent moments so full of truth, love and respect for others, a second movement of the soul can bring us to overcome this holding back of ourselves which took over so quickly and which could again jeopardize our marital happiness. Because of such moments we have come to experience much more than a wonderful marriage – we have come through each other, to experience God himself.[13]

The ideals of what being "one flesh" could mean still have to be worked out in the daily grind of living out our human lives in the fallen world, within the framework of our brokenness as human beings. But if we learn to pray as St Francis of Assisi did, God will hear and answer our prayers, and we will find he changes us beyond recognition. In St Francis' words, we too can pray: "Lord, grant that I may seek more to understand than to be understood."

Cultivating such an attitude opens a door of new hope to us for our marriages.

Chapter 8

"Spring is in the air!" says the radio disc jockey. And he is referring not to brilliant blue skies and sunshine, nor bird songs as nestlings hatch, nor to the splashes of colour dancing over the brown earth of gardens barren from winter's cold. He and his listeners know perfectly well that this is the time when "a young man's thoughts turn to love".

Romantic love flourishes in the atmosphere of the creative beauty of nature in springtime – and romantic love rapidly turns to a man's normal sexual drives aching to find expression and an outlet in union with the woman he loves.

In the Bible, the Song of Solomon shines with the pure beauty of sexual love as God intended it to be experienced, and "displays a profound understanding and celebration of that love which exists between a man and a woman", says Morgan Derham. "This beautiful poetry expresses most vividly that deep primal hunger of the human spirit for that other person with whom he or she can enjoy true intimacy."[1]

In his Scripture Union notes on the Song of Solomon, Morgan Derham highlights some of love's endearing aspects. There is the miracle of the human voice – so designed by God that no two voices are the same. It is often the voice of the loved one which causes the lover's heart to miss a beat (2:8,14). True love can make even the toughest men sensitive to the smallest gestures, little unexpected gifts, and simple thoughtfulness under whose warming rays love blossoms – and in whose absence love shrivels. Even seemingly trivial thoughtlessness can lead to the withering of the fragile plant of developing romantic love (2:15).

Continuing through the Song of Solomon, Morgan Derham points out:

> Love's vision is totally compelling (4:1–7, 9–15). "There is no flaw in you" (4:7). Detail by detail the lover sees perfection in the body of the beloved; there is nothing prurient or corrupt about this – only to those who have lost the ability to contemplate God's creation with wondering and accepting eyes . . . It does no harm for lovers to express these feelings to each other. The cynic will insist that in the cold light of reality the beloved is just another human being, not all that different from the other billion and a half men or women in the world. But this only emphasizes the need for that intimacy within which a man and a woman see and appreciate each other for the distinctive and special creatures that they really are.

He adds that Charles Williams used to say that when we are in love we see one another as Adam and Eve saw each other before the Fall, and as we shall see one another in heaven. If you've been in love then you will know exactly what he means! The other person embodies all that is really lovely, physically, mentally, emotionally and often spiritually. The particular blindness of "love is blind" imparts a sense of wonder and awe that this other person who has been given as an undeserved gift actually reciprocates love. He or she is also blinded to flaws and observant only of that which is truly beautiful in the other.

The fact that this book, the Song of Solomon, is contained in the canon of sacred Scripture indicates the intrinsic value God places on sexual love, and on its rightful expression.

"But you've got it wrong", I can almost hear my friend

Mark chiding me. "Sex is for getting babies. Anything else is just men gratifying their sexual appetites – and that is intrinsically debased and sub-Christian."

No matter how long I spend arguing with Mark, I cannot convince him of what I believe to be the truth as contained in the Bible. It seems that Mark is well and truly trapped within a cage of restricted thinking, coming from his particular small segment of the Church. He is apparently unable to allow himself to open his eyes, read Scripture as a whole and genuinely seek to hear what the Holy Spirit might be wanting to say to him. He represents a vocal minority in current British Christian culture.

To Mark, every advertisement of women dressed scantily, every pair of female legs in front of him on the escalator on the tube, every sight of women's underwear or nighties on display in the shop window are, in his own words, "a cause of temptation". His masculine sexuality comes into play at such sights, he is often aroused sexually and claims: "That is sinful!" He sometimes goes even further and says: "That is lusting after a woman with my eyes – and Jesus said that was as bad as the act of adultery itself."

In fact, Mark rarely responds to such arousals. He immediately thinks of something else and his desire is quenched. He does not share what happens to him with his wife, and so she has no idea that part of him (he daren't admit it) would like his wife to arouse him sexually, so that he could find fulfilment in her other than at set times, in set routines, which give little real pleasure to either of them. If only she knew his problems, she could help him face them by being a foil to them herself.

Sadly, Mark is totally unable to see that sexuality is one of God's greatest gifts to mankind. Was he able to be ruthlessly honest with himself (which he is not), he would realize that deeply engrained in his thinking is an attitude of despising the human body and its needs. And from that attitude stems an unconscious rejection of the marvel of how God made man in Jesus Christ, and of God's creative handiwork in making men and women with bodies designed intricately and beautifully to express their sexuality, in a way that is pure and totally lovely. From his unconscious rejection of the body, and his view of it as intrinsically evil, flows a strict and narrow rejection of sex for any purpose other than producing children.

He is able to justify his attitude by the words: "Look at pornography and the way that mankind has debased sex. Surely that proves that Christians who are called to be 'in the world but not of it' should keep right away from such evil. The Bible says: 'Do not love the world or anything in the world. If anyone loves the world, the love of the Father is not in him. For everything in the world – the cravings of sinful man, the lust of his eyes and the boasting of what he has and does – comes not from the Father but from the world'" (1 John 2:15).

Yet this right teaching that Christians are to avoid corruption must be held within the tension of walking the tightrope of fully appreciating those things which the Bible says have come from God "who richly provides us with everything for our enjoyment" (1 Timothy 6:17). Often it is our misuse of God's wonderful gift of sexuality that is wrong, not the fact that we have received this gift with rejoicing!

Some Christians find that our culture's debasement of sexuality has created within them a repugnance for anything that is to do with sex. One visit to the local sex shop is enough to make many strong men feel sick and degraded. One wadge of unsolicited pornographic magazines through the door with the day's mail is enough to make some feel such overwhelming lust that they hate themselves for that within them which has unexpectedly revealed itself. It turns some away from their wives and from the normal, pure sexual activity to which they are accustomed. One session of viewing so-called "video-nasties" (in order to understand the cancer in our society which harms young children far more than grown adults, and is probably responsible for more sexual and violent crimes than we realize) leaves many men feeling tainted and dirty. The scenes of gang rape, of pain-inflicted sexual intercourse, of women brutally being used as nothing other than the means by which men's lust is satiated, of "group sex", of the cruelty of children being used to satisfy men's abnormal desires, of bestiality and so on, may, to a man's horror, arouse him so powerfully sexually that he feels filthy and hates that which he discovers such materials can drag out of him.

The availability and commonness of "soft porn" in newsagents' shops, and the fact that "hard porn" is sometimes left on tubes, or on seats by bus stops, means that many in their lives come across pictures which they have no desire to see but cannot avoid glancing at. The sense of repugnance that they feel for themselves and for their reactions and arousal by such material, may lead some men to feel that they cannot possibly come close to their wife, who is so pure and lovely, and who (he assumes) could not possibly know about such things.

"My husband's an elder in our church, and everyone thinks the world of him," Elizabeth told me. "I just don't know what to do. The other day I was clearing out our bedroom and turned over the mattress, and there under it were these pornographic magazines. When I asked him about them, he said he didn't know who'd put them there . . ."

Celia shared: "Before my husband became a Christian, he couldn't have sex with me unless he got turned-on by girly magazines. Now he's a Christian he knows it's wrong, but we don't know how to stop it. It seems that's the only way he can make love to me . . ."

"I wish my wife would help me, but I daren't ask for

help," Anthony said. "The only way I can make love to her is to imagine that she's wearing really frilly things instead of her cotton nightie . . . and usually when I start doing that I find I'm imagining someone else and not thinking of her, which I know isn't right . . ."

These three represent but a few of many who have talked to me about the effect that our culture's obsession with sex has had on their intimate lives. They have allowed what is going on around them to contaminate their own sex lives, until they have reached a point where the Holy Spirit has had to begin to convince them that something is not working as God planned.

The thrilling thing for Christians is that Jesus Christ can free us from any kind of slavery – including that in which spoiled sex may bind us. There are Christian counsellors available who can help talk through these problems and who are not shocked by anything they may hear. They are only too well aware that the Church is now gaining members who are the products of the permissive society and have been taught by it that "anything goes as long as you both like it", and who now long to be freed from slavery to some activities which they sense are not God's best and most beautiful for them.

For each person feeling tainted by sexual perversion comes the Bible's healing and cleansing words: "If we confess our sins, he is faithful and just and will forgive us our sins and purify us from all unrighteousness" (1 John 1:9).

Along with this, today's Christian leaders must have the courage to stand out and proclaim: "Perverted sex is not what God intends. A man should be aroused by his wife and by her alone, without the need for external stimuli . . . anything else makes a mockery of sexual intercourse as symbolizing the union between the two and turns it into a mechanical performance that can be initiated by the right 'key' which winds up the man and woman like clockwork toys and makes them perform their prescribed roles."

Definition of perversion is harder and Christian opinion differs. It ranges from a majority who would agree that any sexual activity that is accompanied by the deliberate giving or receiving of pain is off-centre when it comes to normality ratings; any sexual activity that is not private and is not exclusive to the married couple alone is also out; and sexual activity involving a member of the same sex is likewise forbidden. Other areas where disagreement exists as to what is permissible for the Christian couple include, for some, oral sex, and for others mutual or solitary masturbation.

Guidelines that the Christian can apply in his or her own life are sometimes hard to define. The Bible does not give clear commands in all cases as to what types of sexual expression are acceptable for Christians and what are not. It is clear that sexual intercourse is to be reserved for marriage alone. Clearly forbidden are incest, rape, adultery, fornication, and physical expression of homosexual or lesbian attraction, desire or love. What is, or is not, acceptable *within* the marriage is nowhere defined in words of one syllable. To discern this, we need to understand biblical *principles*. Central must be Jesus' command to "love your neighbour as yourself" (Luke 10:27).

The Christian's closest neighbour is his marriage partner, to whom nothing must be done that could cause hurt in any way. If your partner is reluctant about something that would bring you sexual pleasure, then refraining from that activity is expressing Jesus' love. And so is refraining from requesting it! If something actually hurts your partner physically or emotionally, but is necessary for you to obtain sexual satisfaction, then I believe that out of love you should refrain from doing it. Possibly you should seek skilled help in learning how to be fulfilled sexually without needing to resort to doing something that hurts your partner.

You may have a very generous partner who is trying to love you fully and please you in every possible way. Be careful not to exploit this by letting your partner make love in a way that is slightly, or very, repugnant to him or her – simply to give you pleasure and fulfilment.

Jesus also commands us to "Love each other as I have loved you. Greater love has no one than this, that one lay down his life for his friends" (John 15:12–13). Where sexual satisfaction is a purely selfish thing and gives nothing to the other person, it fails to reflect the selfless love which Jesus longs to see in the lives of his children. Some people regard masturbation as no more than selfishness, and as something that should be stopped because it gives nothing to the one who is loved and is a private activity of self-gratification. Others would disagree with this and state that "masturbation is God's gift to men"!

Linda and Robert found in their love-making that God seemed to be at the very centre of their bodies as they joined in the physical act of loving one another. It was natural, as they lay satisfied – still united – in one another's arms, for them to pray and talk, and thank the God who had made them in such a way to enjoy a foretaste of heaven in the union of their bodies. "But," explained Linda, "as we were married longer and began to experiment with different things the books said you could do when you made love, we found there were some things for which we could *not* thank God . . . and it was then that we realized that those particular activities were wrong for us."

A conscience, kept alert by daily prayer, communion with God, and reading God's Word, is one of the most helpful guides as to what is wrong and what is right for each Christian couple. A good rule is, "If in doubt, don't!"

Many have found, to their cost, that sexual experimentation has led them from one experience to another, and each has been slightly less within normal boundaries than the one before. Without noticing it they have slipped down a slope and into the mud at the bottom. "The books told us not to be ashamed of our bodies and so we weren't", said Joan. "That was liberating. But then, as we tried out lots of different things, we found that over the course of several years we had got right away from the normal kind of sex we used to practise when we were first married. We had to get it all sorted out with God and with each other – and that was really painful. It was difficult to get back to normal and find ordinary sex fulfilling . . . and we didn't, until we stopped regarding each other as objects to satisfy us sexually and saw one another as total people again."

As long as a marriage is held together by a very strong sexual bond and weak real love, it faces potential danger. Thielicke says:

> *Agape* does not take the place of *eros* but rather takes it into its service and leads me to love the other person in the milieu of the erotic, and in an erotic way, just as I love him in other areas of life in another way . . .
>
> If, however, the marriage is founded exclusively upon this erotic principle, then it will be subjected to permanent crises, for it will repeatedly be compelled to ask: "Is this person really the 'right one' for me?" . . . This results in something like a permanent compulsion to keep watch on whether the other person is still capable of functioning . . . Thus, often enough in the merely erotic, the merely "romantic" marriage, the honeymoon is followed by a crisis. With deadly certainty the moment comes in such marriages when the comparison of one's own partner with another, and especially younger representatives of his or her sex, turns out to be a disadvantage, and then the half-solution (like infidelity) or the radical solution (like divorce) is sought for.[2]

Grasping some of the fundamental differences between a woman's sexual make-up and that of a man is vital for all couples as they learn to love in the way in which God intended them to. Built into the make-up of a woman is that which makes her loving a part of her total life and not a separate, well-defined compartment which can be isolated from the rest of her. Love constitutes the whole of life for most women. It is not something that can be isolated for after 11.00 p.m. and confined to the bedroom. Her sexual experience takes place within the framework of living in harmony with her husband, understanding him and being understood by him, talking and sharing with him and knowing that a lasting affection exists between them even though the flame of sexual passion may have flickered to embers years earlier.

Paul Tournier explains:

> The wife has an emotional need, which often the husband fails to recognize. She needs to hear tender words, she needs to go out with her husband, to share excitement with him as they admire something, to experience deep oneness with him in the silent moments of exaltation. For her, love means a high level of affection, this is why she would like her husband to be with her always. She counts the hours he gives her, the Sundays he spends with her, the evenings he takes her out. This for her is the way that love is expressed.[3]

On the other hand, a man tends to live for his work and for the power and the success that he gains through it. Love is shut away in the "home" compartment of his mind and does not preoccupy his thoughts when he is at work. When he is at home with his wife his sexual desire may suddenly rise . . . the glimpse of her legs, an evocative tune on the radio, the scent of her perfume . . . and he crushes her to him wanting instant sexual union. If she complies, he will probably take her and satisfy his overwhelming need, and may then sit up with the words: "Where's supper? I'm starving!" His wife will be stunned by his words. She, unlike him, will long for him to continue holding her, murmuring their private words of love and helping her to reach a sexual climax. She will often want to stay like this with him for a long time – while he, satisfied, thinks of his empty stomach! Leaving her to accuse him with the words: "You don't really love me, do you? All you want is my body."

Tournier explains:

All of which means that she cannot understand this masculine form of love, impulsive and of short duration. She would like her husband to love her as she does him, tenderly and continually. Such a lack of understanding can lead a wife as far as to feel complete disgust for sexual union. That he should wish to have union with her when they have hardly cooled off from a heated argument is quite impossible for her to understand.[4]

Understanding is vital on both sides, and real love makes allowances for the differences between the sexes and for the other's needs and manners.

"I learned", said Judy, "to let Mike make love to me the minute he got home if he wanted to. There were times when things had been so bad at work that he had to express his frustration and anger somehow, and for him the way to do it was through sexual intercourse. I never felt very loved after those times, but I did feel that I had been able to give him a gift only I could give, and one that I could choose to give or withhold as he would never force himself on me. It worked, too! When it was like that, later on in the evening he'd start to court me and spend all the time I needed to be ready for him. When it came to the second time round on those evenings, then I'd feel like his queen, loved, cherished, and satisfied totally due to the time and care he put into making sure that I was being fulfilled."

David learned another lesson. "The more I tried to have sex with Sally, the more she found reasons why I couldn't. I got really fed-up about it. She said I was highly sexed and she couldn't keep up with me. But I think I only wanted her about four times a week. Then, I found out how men and women differed. That was the first time I realized that Sally wasn't rejecting *me*, and that I wasn't making sex anything that she could write home about. I started trying to be more affectionate – you know, phoning home during the day to see if she was all right, leaving her a little note in the breadbin to say I loved her, buying her just one red rose or a small bunch of freesias, taking out the rubbish without being asked to, complimenting her on how she looked and what she did . . . and I found that she began to cuddle up to me as we watched TV instead of sitting on the other side of the room. Then I found that she liked me caressing her, how we did when we were courting. At that time I'd thought that was as far as we could go before marriage – I never thought that it could be part of her getting ready for intercourse in marriage itself.

"If I played with her breasts and thighs when we were doing the washing-up, I found she liked it as long as I didn't try to have her there and then . . . and that was hard for me as it aroused me fast . . . but, when I was patient and got her wanting me as much as I wanted her, then we started to have really good sex. I found it was worth slowing down to her pace, because we were both satisfied then. And she stopped saying I was 'sex mad' like she did before . . ."

Within the security of a loving relationship, it is vital for a couple to share the things in love-making that they do or do not like, what turns them on or damps them down. Words like "Touch me here . . . it makes me tingle all over . . .", "Don't mention the children coming in or I'm switched off . . .", "When you do that I want you so desperately I could die . . ." must never be taboo. Within the privacy of the bedroom a couple must talk freely and use words that are not used in public, so that each can teach the other how to make their expression of mutual love as satisfying and as fulfilling as God intends them to make it. Puritanical silence with one's marriage partner can lead to lack of communication about one of those areas in marriage where straight and loving talking is most needed. That it is biblical to talk about matters like this, is eloquently expressed in the Song of Solomon — where there is a gentle blend of sensual speech, reticence, erotic words and modesty.

The couple who are able to speak to one another in private of their own love-making are the more able to share with their children the joys of sex — and so sex education is not dad summoning son into the study for an artificial talk about the birds and bees! Parents who manage to talk freely to one another about the subject find that they are also able to talk easily and naturally to their children.

This has a further bonus, in that the man who is able to talk to his wife about his sexuality is then able to share any sexual temptations he may face with her. Paul Tournier says:

Many wives find it hard to understand that their husbands can be tempted sexually . . . she thinks that if he really loved her, he wouldn't think of other women. Whereas, it is precisely because of his love for her that he confides in her. He feels misunderstood, condemned and despised. He withdraws into himself. Henceforth he will avoid all such confidences which can only cast a shadow on their marital unity. Yet, the veil of silence may well jeopardize their marriage far more than his sex drive. The best protection is to be able to speak honestly

110

of them and to find in the wife understanding, without any trace of complicity whatsoever, effective and affective help needed to overcome them.

To a man, his wife may appear

> ... as a policeman, an incarnation of the moral law ... nevertheless, even in his sensual temptations, as in his deviations from honesty or lack of humility, a man can be helped only if he feels understood and accepted, as he is with all his misery. Such generous acceptance then is for him a reflection of the mercy of God. For God loves us not for our virtues but for our needs.[5]

In a society in which sex screams at you from most advertisement hoardings, from magazines, papers, shops, TV and radio, you would think that people would be free of problems about sex. Yet, the devaluation of sex and its misuse for purposes other than that for which God originally designed it, has turned God's most precious gift to us into one which leads many of us into the most problematical areas of our lives and relationships.

In closing his notes on the Song of Solomon, Morgan Derham says:

> Because love is as "strong as death", because it meets such a fundamental human need, love can all too easily "flip over" and become as destructive as it was constructive, as cruel as it was tender. It is here that we put Solomon's Song into its biblical context, and remind ourselves of that which God has planted as the supreme "sign" of human experience – the cross. Divine love, however rejected, however abused, however hurt, never turns bitter, never ceases to pray and care for those who reject it. And that is the ultimate in loving.[6]

Many couples walk out on one another when things do not work out sexually as the manuals teach they should. Many give up trying, and look for other partners or other ways of sublimating their sexual urges. God's way for his children is for them to love through sexual difficulties, because of them, and despite them. And through all this to come to a greater understanding of one another, of love, and of how to make their relationship the kind that God designed it to be.

The cross in the Protestant Church is an empty cross, and the tomb an empty tomb – signifying that through his resurrection Jesus Christ has overcome the forces of the evil one who seeks to ruin God's plans for mankind. God has redeemed us – fallen humanity – with our brokenness and fallen sexuality. In God's hands we can experience the redemption of even this part of our humanity. Our sexuality can be transformed so that with our partners we begin to reflect the loving relationship that exists within the Godhead as Father, Son and Holy Spirit live in union and communion with each other. And that for us can be a foretaste of the bliss of heaven.

Chapter 9

If, for one reason or another, your marriage partner is unable to meet all the needs you expect or hope that he or she will meet in your life, then how far can you go in pursuing a relationship (not involving sexual infidelity) with another person without betraying your partner?

This question is asked by many but answered by few! There are few Christians who have either the opportunity or the courage to share the way in which they have survived the involvement of a third person in their marriage, especially when the presence of that third person has in some way caused them problems.

Joanna shared her story in writing:

I propped my dripping umbrella against the door. It was then that I noticed the mail lying undisturbed on the floor. I was enveloped by a now familiar, but curious feeling of hope mixed with fear. Picking up the post, I wondered briefly why letters always seem to fall face down – as though trying to keep their secrets for as long as possible, by making it difficult for the receiver to recognize at a glance neat typewritten labels or the familiar sprawling hand of a friend.

But the letter I anticipated that threatened to disturb me wasn't there, and I was cross with myself for letting my feelings get the better of me. Putting the kettle on I opened an envelope with a neat, almost sterile look to it – and was surprised by its contents. The envelope was addressed in anonymous black capitals and inside was a card. Words by author John Powell read: "The loving hand of God is forever touching our lives, but there are certain moments when he touches us in a very special way and raises us to new heights of love if we are open and willing. Sometimes there are moments of struggle when the Lord's invitation is to grow. His challenge is to really believe that new life can be born from our difficulties, our hardships, our sufferings. When we win little triumphs of strength and love, God widens our hearts and our worlds and our lives."[1]

I read it again and again, wondering as I did who could have sent such a card and got the timing so right. I felt moved and loved, and held tight for a moment – pulling the warmth of it round me like a cloak, drawing comfort from the reassurance it offered.

The months have passed, but I still grieve the death of a friendship – wondering with each delivery of mail, every telephone call, whether this might be the time we discover that more can be said. It is almost as if I refuse to believe that our friendship has actually died, but instead merely lives in a coma, awaiting the discovery of some miracle, life-giving cure.

It had been an unusual friendship. The differences in background and temperament should have distanced us. Instead we found common ground in our Christian faith, and for a time delighted in a friendship/love relationship as described so completely by C. S. Lewis: "This love, free from all duties but those which love has freely assumed ... is the sort of love one can imagine between angels."

It was a friendship which neither of us had expected and was all the more cherished because we believed it to be a gift from God. On the face of it we had little in common. I was the child of a broken home. My parents had divorced and each remarried, so that I grew up with two sets of parents, but no real sense of belonging. I left school at fifteen with no qualifications. But now I am happily married, and have found security and a sense of belonging with my husband and children.

My Christian experience is very real. It is a practical Christianity that accepts this seeming round of non-events as what God has planned for my life for the moment, so that marriage and motherhood have so far been the happiest of adventures.

Martin came into all of this as a newly married, ill-at-ease curate in his first parish. His childhood had been settled and almost privileged. As an only child, his parents had been devoted to his well-being and dedicated to his education. His academic diplomas and achievements are a fitting testimony to his determination not to let them down. But clever, serious and sensitive as he is, his sheltered past had left him as sadly lacking in experience of real life as I am in academic qualifications.

It was the gradual realization of how much we could learn from one another that initially was the main thrust in our friendship. I borrowed his books and we discussed theology. He asked my advice on some of the real-life situations he faced and furthered his ministry. Surprisingly the relationship balanced perfectly, and with time and care developed into something very special.

With hindsight you could argue that our relationship had been one of need, with each of us looking to the other to fill deficiency in our lives. This may have been true, but it had been founded on a common interest and built on honesty and mutual trust.

C. S. Lewis again wrote: "You will not find the warrior, the poet, the philosopher or the Christian by staring in his eyes as if he were your mistress: better fight beside him, read with him, argue with him, pray with him."

And that was how it had been. We made one another

laugh as well as cry. There were difficult moments and times of tenderness. Some things were better said with touch than with word.

We were Christian friends, acknowledging the love between us and thanking God for it – all the time agreeing that, as friends, we had no exclusive rights or claims on one another, and no rights of possession. Those belonged to our respective spouses – who had been more than gracious in their understanding of our relationship.

But the time came when we needed to ask ourselves a question, and the answer changed everything: "Is this relationship," we queried, "meaningful though it is, in danger of becoming an affair of the heart, a third-party relationship that will be a betrayal of the trust our loved ones have placed in us?"

It was difficult to answer, and the dilemma Martin and I found ourselves in was further complicated by the knowledge that the society in which we live has little understanding of male/female relationships without romantic involvement – thus every moment of tenderness or open show of affection was open to misinterpretation.

There were no set guidelines, no published rules of conduct. It was a matter of conscience to distinguish between tenderness and intimacy, the sensitive touch of a friend and the sensual caress of a lover.

The parting when it came was sudden and final. With two marriages and the feelings of so many people at stake, there could be no room for doubt.

Now miles and pain distance my friend and me, more effectively than our strange pasts ever could. All that is left is memory – fragments like autumn leaves, the last untidy remnants of the past glorious summer.

So, I mourn, not the loss of a loved one through death but the bewildering loss of a friend through the death of a friendship. I grieve, that one, once so loved, is no longer part of my life.

The sorrow I feel isn't that of bereavement, nor contrition for a wrong act that has taken away my self-respect or innocence, but the poignant sense of loneliness that I can hardly put into words. I never had or wanted a lover, but I did have and wanted – and still yearn for – the love of my friend.

As with any failed relationship, much is left to forgive and be forgiven. Any attempt at communication has been so painful that now all we require of one another is silence. The hope I sometimes feel when I scan the mail or answer the telephone is shortlived and sadly turns to fear and further hurt – which threatens to rob me of the will to try again. But I know that ultimately my hope is in Christ. I believe that this difficult experience has been for my own good.

It is ironic that it was Martin who introduced me to the gentle writings of John Powell. Perhaps it is fitting that I should draw comfort from his words now and reply to the card I received today.

I feel I can say, "Thank you God for touching my life in this special way and teaching me new heights of love. I have struggled. But I believe I have grown; help me to appreciate the new life that will be born of my difficulties and suffering. In your strength and through your love, I will continue to believe that knowing Martin has widened my heart and enriched my life. And so I will not give up on friendship – it is too rare and precious a gift."

But there is just one thing. I wish I knew who sent that card. It has helped to know of someone, who, seeing my sorrow, offered me understanding, so that I have felt able to share my experience – and have benefited so much from the sense of freedom this has brought.[2]

117

There are, of course, two sides to any account like this one, and I invited a husband whose wife had a similar relationship to the one above to pretend that he was the one who had dropped that card through Joanna's letterbox, and to write her a reply based on how he felt when his wife was doing the same thing. This is what he had to say:

She should have read the card by now – I dropped it through the door at lunchtime. I hope it brings her warmth, a sense of hope and purpose . . . to know that someone identifies with her pain. Even though we are separated by circumstance.

Years on it can still hurt occasionally. But it is a familiar pain now, and the joy I have known since that time is a welcome reminder of how tiny scars can conceal what were once gaping wounds.

We had been married for six years when their friendship began almost imperceptibly. Rebecca and I were happy – our children too. We were committed to each other, our God, our community, and our church. I thought we were as content and fulfilled as possible this side of heaven. I don't know when I first realized that we were no longer just a wide, devoted fellowship. But I suddenly realized that he and Rebecca would regularly be locked in deep, laughing, intense discussions, oblivious to everyone else. His name and views often came up in our conversations.

Of course I knew that we didn't have exclusive rights on each other. We both accepted that we could not – nor should want to – fulfil each other completely. Only God could do that, and the outworking of our relationship with him through others.

But although they were never lovers in the physical sense, as time went on I came to feel betrayed in the empty, numbing way which probably only those whose partners have swapped their marriage bed for another's can really understand. It hurt insistently – the awareness that she felt that there was something very intimate and important missing from our relationship that she could find only with another man.

I wasn't the jealous type who refused to let her go out alone. We had wide and varied friendships in our community. But this was so different. I trusted her, yet I couldn't accept it. Much as I tried, my fears and insecurities would not stay buried.

It had to affect our relationship, and it did. I didn't want her to know how I felt because it seemed somehow unreasonable. But the fact that something was wrong was evident in so many ways. Her bewilderment that I should feel as I did only worsened the tensions.

I still believe – though she would probably deny it . . . indeed, I doubt if she was even aware of it – that there was a romantic ingredient in their friendship. The excitement of sharing deep and open truths with each other, of exploring anew, thinking, probing . . . I can understand the emotional pull. I realized how often I had failed to stimulate the discovering aspect of our marriage in the last few years.

My culpability didn't ease the pain, for a while we struggled to pretend we were being understanding of each other's reluctance or inability to be accepting, trusting, sensitive to the other's feelings.

It didn't end; just sort of faded away. Over months, then years, the intensity passed. During that time we both learned much about God's love, patience, assurance. And through it all we still loved each other desperately.

I'm glad it happened, though the hurt was real and lasting. Through it we both have grown. As Christians, as friends, as parents – and ultimately closer together.

We were both right, we were both wrong; it was a curious mix of attitudes and opinions.

And while I cannot empathize with Joanna – I can identify. The pain is no less real because it is experienced by the "opponent". I hope she understands. It's not what is lost, but what is found in the process that is important.

Only sometimes when Rebecca bursts in through the front door bubbling and bright, or talks earnestly on the phone, or seems lost in her own thoughts, I'll take myself back to those days. Like tracing a finger over a small, silvery-white thread of flesh; all that remains of the knitting together of the closeness of brokenness.

As John Powell said: "Sometimes there are moments of struggle, when the Lord's invitation is to grow." I hope Joanna understands this.[3]

Chapter 10

Most of us really do mean it when we promise to be faithful to our marriage partners. We take our marriage vows seriously. "Bedhopping" or sleeping around is out. And in that solemn moment, standing in church before the minister, making lifelong promises, we have no intention of breaking them.

But many Christians find that the temptation to adultery is one that catches them unawares, totally to their surprise, and stumbles them. They never meant it, they did not plan for their friendship with someone else to go as far as it has. Yet they find they have fallen into a trap from which it seems impossible to extricate themselves without causing untold sufferings.

The deep friendship that began as companionship developed into "only a close friendship", then turned into a sexual encounter when both were off their guard. This happens more commonly than many Christians either care or dare to admit. Some have written to unburden themselves and to tell me of their experiences in this. One woman shared with me:

> I had this really good friend. He talked to me and treated me in ways that my husband didn't. He understood me and almost read my thoughts. My cares and concerns were his too. We really were moved by the same things and cared deeply about some issues about which my husband was totally indifferent. In this man's friendship I found a source of strength and courage to do certain things I felt God wanted me to do.
>
> My husband didn't even really seem to notice what

was going on. He didn't particularly mind my having this friendship. I got the impression that he didn't particularly care one way or the other. It gave him a quiet life!

Over the years this particular man's support increasingly meant more to me. He stood by me when I was hurt, he prayed with and for me, and he gave me the mental and emotional courage that I needed to go on. I always longed that my husband would be the person to give me this quality of support. But he wasn't bothered. And he even said one or twice: "It's great – you've got Jim, and he can give you the kind of support that I can't."

Jim and I were increasingly thrown together, until we realized one day that our friendship was verging on being exclusive. And when that happened, without explanation, Jim walked out of my life. And it was about eight years before I saw him again, close enough to be able to talk to him about what had happened. Those eight years taught me things that I hadn't realized about myself. When Jim disappeared I grieved the loss of a friend who supported and encouraged me . . . but it took me about four years to realize that I had loved Jim in a way that was more than friendship. I suppose if I am absolutely honest I have to admit that I was "in love" with Jim.

One of the toughest things I have ever had to face as a Christian was that I had fallen in love with someone other than my husband. And before God, as I thought and prayed about it over the months, I knew that not only must I admit the truth but I had to face the reality of it. I, who thought I was a fortress and above such things as that, had been "in love" with someone else.

She continued:

Perhaps that wouldn't have mattered as much as it did if I hadn't let Jim take over much of my thinking. Much of my creativity and the kind of person I was had been derived from the input that he was giving into my life. It never entered my head to think in terms of going to bed with him – although I must have been aware of the danger because I was always careful to dress in a way that was not provocative sexually when he was around. I knew that if I ever had an affair with him it would end the friendship that was very precious to me.

The more I thought about it over the months the more I realized that I had given Jim the love that should have gone to my husband. I had actually deprived my husband of the caring and attention that should have been his. The fact that he didn't seem to mind that having happened, and was apparently happy for Jim to fill a void in my life, wasn't particularly relevant in the kind of sorting out of myself that had to be done on my knees before the cross. Not only did I have to admit to myself that I had been in love with somebody else, but I had to repent before God that I had been unfaithful to my husband in every way except actual sexual infidelity – Jim and I had never got close enough even to hold hands!

All this was hard for me to sort out and took ages. I was angry with my husband for not trying to meet my needs himself and for giving me his blessing in going to another man to fill my life as he himself – as my husband – should have done. I was angry that my husband didn't seem to be bothered that he wasn't meeting those needs, and didn't seem concerned enough to understand me himself and try to be the kind of man who would give me the sort of nourishment and sustenance that Jim gave me.

And I was very angry with God for allowing me, when I was in my late teens, to marry a man who could not understand my needs, nor show me his, so that there could be no real relationship of reciprocal sharing, caring and meeting one another's needs – which I believed to be the essence of Christian marriage.

But time taught me that Jim had been right to make the hard break of walking out of our relationship. He resisted my attempts to drag him back by simply switching off to me – he was never unkind, just unresponsive.

I have never felt so alone or so bereft as I did when Jim was no longer part of me. I used to look at those cards in shops with the words: "Better to have loved and lost than never to have loved." I thought, "How stupid!" I wished I had never loved this man for then I would never have had to live through the pain of being separated from him.

But gradually, as I realized that he really was gone, I have found that I needed to discover peace within the deepest parts of my soul, and healing for the hurt at the loss of him, and the bereavement of facing the fact that it was highly unlikely that I was ever going to have a husband who would fulfil my expectations of marriage. And, being the kind of person I am, I needed to tie all this up in symbolic action.

Once on a day out, Jim and I had together visited a tiny chapel in the countryside and wandered round reading inscriptions on the gravestones. There was one extraordinary one with his name on it. And the date of his birth was given as the date of the death of his unknown namesake. That grave was in one of the loveliest parts of the country, and in my own symbolic way I laid my friendship to rest in that grave.

It was one blustery autumn day when I went back by myself and slipped into the silent chapel carrying a single deep-red rose. I lit the candles on the altar, and as they flickered in the gloom I could not stop weeping, desperately trying to pray, shivering with cold and emotion: "Loving heavenly Father, I have loved one who was not mine to love. I have sinned in giving my marriage love to another person. I repent of this sin and come to you asking for forgiveness."

And looking up at the gentle eyes of the Man who hung on the cross, I knew that he understood. It didn't matter whether I had sinned or had been sinned against by a husband who didn't seem really to love me. What did matter was that I now knew that I had been wrong, and I came to the cross to confess my wrong and seek forgiveness at the feet of Jesus. And from that cross came the biblical words of reassurance: "If we confess our sins he is faithful and just to forgive us our sins and to cleanse us from all unrighteousness."

As I sobbed out my heart in pain in the seclusion of that tiny chapel, I knew in the innermost part of my being that God had accepted me and loved me, and that it was all right.

I pulled my heavy coat round me and slipped out to the gravestone. During the summer months the weeds had sprouted and nettles had grown tall and vicious over the earth on that grave. I rolled up the sleeves of my coat and plunged my arms into the nettles, grabbing them and ripping them out in some kind of self-inflicted injury to atone for my sin, and their acid sting bit through my thin blouse and pained my arms for days.

When my work was done, and the grave was cleared and tended so that it looked as if someone who loved had come to wait and weep a while, I lifted my single red rose to my lips and laid it with a kiss of love and farewell on the soft brown earth. "Goodbye, my darling", I whispered and ran blindly to the car to return home and away from the emotion of that day. Back to the laundry that needed sorting and potatoes that needed peeling for supper for six.

That ritual in some significant way laid my friendship to rest and buried it along with the one whose namesake I would never know.

Then I found I had deliberately to shut Jim out of my thinking. It was hard. There were times when I'd wake with frightening nightmares that Jim had left me. There were times when I would wake in the middle of the night and find I was thinking about him. But gradually over the months my dreams stopped being centred around Jim.

Once when my husband invited him round to lunch, I found I was thrown and suddenly unable to cope emotionally. I wasn't ready to meet him socially yet. But, at least I had faced the fact that I had been in love with this man, and that our relationship had to be over – so meeting him as if we were mere social acquaintances over lunch helped me face reality.

A few years later we found ourselves as the only two attending a committee meeting – the others had sent apologies. He made some comment about, "Those years when we used to see so much of one another . . ." I found myself softly saying, "I was in love with you, you know . . ." He smiled. "I guessed as much . . ." And, after that, I was at peace. He no longer haunted me at unexpected moments, nor did thoughts of him wake me from sleep, nor did certain pieces of music remind me of him and the pain of being apart from him.

Others have shared similar stories with me of the way in which they have found a relationship with someone of the opposite sex going far beyond that which they felt was in keeping with their marriage vows made before God. Emotional, intellectual and spiritual infidelity are but a stone's throw away from sexual infidelity. They come close to Jesus' words about those who, looking on a woman lustfully, have already committed adultery with her in their hearts. Yet many of us Christians fail to recognize the subtlety of this.

I do not know of any simple way in which the man or

woman who wants to stay faithful in every way to his or her life partner can know where the fine borderline lies between a healthy and good relationship and actually being "in love".

I have sat down with friends and we have tried to draw up warning lists. We have come up with thoughts like – take care if you spend more time and trouble dressing to go out with someone other than your marriage partner; beware if you take more delight in choosing just the right present for your friend than you do for your marriage partner; think carefully if you are jealous of your friend's marriage partner and his or her friends; there may be something wrong if you share with your friend things that you wouldn't tell another friend and possibly not even your husband or wife.

Other questions which can be asked with revealingly helpful, if painful, answers, include: Do I wish I had met my friend when we were both younger and free? Would I be happy if my partner developed the kind of relationship with someone else that I have with my friend? Do I compare my partner unfavourably with my friend – emotionally, spiritually, physically? What do my children feel about this friendship – does it make them feel insecure? Is it right for younger married Christians, who may see but know little about my friendship, to develop similar friendships with those of the opposite sex?

If I am dissatisfied with my own marriage relationship, am I still totally committed to making it richer and more fulfilling? Have I questioned deeply whether or not my partner's apparent willingness to allow my friendship to continue is covering a hurt he or she may not be able to share?

Am I sexually attracted to my friend? Have I the courage to talk to a mature Christian friend about this relationship – on the understanding that the advice given may be a call to halt it before too many people get hurt?[1]

In today's society in which it would seem that unfaithfulness is considered the norm, all the more must the Christian stand on guard against assaults being made on marriage. If a Christian wants to keep his marriage intact, he can no longer assume that all will automatically be well. This must be fought for and guarded against.

Society has conditioned us to expect more of marriage than former generations expected. Dr Jack Dominian says:

> The ideal of contemporary marriage is indeed lofty. Its consummation needs an equivalent degree of insight and perseverance . . . The personal and sexual world of contemporary marriage has been shaped by a variety of social and psychological factors, which collectively have raised the level of awareness of the meaning of love in marriage.[2]

These high ideals and high expectations are deeply held by many men and women and their lack of realization in their own marriages can be something difficult for them to handle. There is the immense feeling of being let down, of feeling rejected and imperfect, of hopelessness, helplessness and perhaps total defeat. Some may have to face the fact quite objectively that no matter how hard they try, they will never, ever achieve the kind of relationship that they believe is intended by God when a man and a woman truly become one flesh.

The realization that this is not to be, is something that many quite rightly fight against. There is no need to give up hope too soon, and there is every reason to struggle in every possible way to build a marriage relationship that is as rich and as strong as it can possibly be. Quite often, a deliberate effort to learn to communicate and to understand one another will deepen the relationship in an incredible way. A couple may be able to learn to do this on their own, or through sharing with understanding

Christian friends. Others find marriage-enrichment weekends or marriage-enhancement courses help them. Others find that Christian marriage counsellors (though these are few and far between) or the Marriage Guidance Centre are able to help them understand themselves and their relationship in such a way that they are able to begin to build a renewed firm and lasting relationship with one another.

But what of those who have tried? Those who in desperation, with no tears left to flow, and no voice left to cry, gasp: "It's failed . . . it isn't working . . . and we have no hope of making it work . . ."

Do we as Christians turn to one another, if we reach such a position, and gently look our partner in the eye and say: "Thanks for trying so hard. Thanks for all you've tried to do. I'm so sorry it won't work. I'm so sorry we're totally incompatible. We'll have to part"? Is this really the way in which God wants us to go? It is the way of the world, but is this the way of the Bible?

The Bible says:

They asked, "Is it lawful for a man to divorce his wife for any and every reason?"

"Haven't you read," (Jesus) replied, "that at the beginning the Creator 'made them male and female', and said, 'For this reason a man will leave his father and mother and be united to his wife, and the two will become one flesh'? So they are no longer two, but one. Therefore what God has joined together, let man not separate."

"Why then," they asked, "did Moses command that a man give his wife a certificate of divorce and send her away?"

Jesus replied, "Moses permitted you to divorce your wives because your hearts were hard. But it was not this way from the beginning. I tell you that anyone who

129

divorces his wife, except for marital unfaithfulness, and marries another woman commits adultery" (Matthew 19:3–9)

A stage may be reached in some marriages, where each partner knows that the relationship is not working as it should. Sexual unfaithfulness has not entered into their situation, and according to the words of Jesus they have no real grounds for divorce – attractive as the words "breakdown of our relationship" and "incompatible" may sound should a divorce be sought.

Since God himself has joined a couple together, I believe that we must, with his help, fight our utmost to make our marriages work as Christians. For some of us, this may involve being far more realistic about what we expect in marriage. As Dr Jack Dominian continually stresses, modern marriages are built on expectations that exceed those of earlier generations. And with that rise in expectation comes a rise in the divorce rate, for dreams are unfulfilled and hopes and plans are shattered.

Some of us need to face the fact that our marriage is not going to be what we thought it would be. It is not going to be one of those unions "where two hearts beat as one" – both beating in unison to that of the heartbeat of the Creator of the world. We may have dreamed that as Christians we would have all ideals in common, share deeply at a spiritual level, and be like one person working towards a single goal and aim in life. We may have thought that somehow, since we both knew and loved the same Saviour and Master and wanted to do nothing other than serve him all our lives, our marriage relationship had to be as beautiful and as easy as our relationship with him. For many, life is not like that. But good human relationships are built of stern stuff – and the best are those that have stood strong, despite life's storms, misunderstandings, bitter disappointments, and, through adversity, grown from flabbiness to iron-like strength.

To begin with, some of us must stop retreating into fantasy and imagining that our unions could, should, or would ever be what they cannot be. They can only be that which God intends to make of our human clay and that which we allow him to shape us into. And realistically we must face the fact that we bring into our marriages our genetic make-up and the shaping of our personality derived from the experiences through which we have passed as babies and children. These factors may in themselves prevent us, or our partners, from being the kind of people fantasy would like us to be.

Facing facts, reflecting in the cold light of day, assessing things as they really are, we may find we need to admit (perhaps simply in the privacy of our own hearts): "My marriage is not going to be what I thought it had to be in order to succeed . . ." The day we are able to face this fact and stop running away into dreams of what we'd like but can never have, may be one of the days heralding major growth in our lives and marriages.

"OK," we try to be honest with ourselves, "it's never going to be what I thought it should be. Shall I opt out?" For the Christian, one who is living biblically, there is no option at this stage other than to stay in and to work with the raw materials of what does exist to try to build something – even if that something is less than the perfection imagined on the wedding day.

Some Christians who face facts and decide not to opt out, need to take emotional time out of life at this stage in order to absorb what they have discovered about themselves, their partner and their marriage. This is the time to be gentle with yourself and not to make demands on yourself that cannot really be met.

Should you ever face this, then you will be facing a major loss – a kind of bereavement. You are having to face the fact that your marriage is not going to be the relationship that you expected it to be. In almost the same way that the parents of a handicapped child need to be allowed time to mourn the healthy child they did not give birth to, so you need to give yourself the time and space required to grieve the fact that your marriage probably will not be what you expected. The relationship you anticipated has gone from your grasp, and if you remain faithful to your partner it is unlikely that you will ever have a relationship where your soul is so merged with another that you are truly "one flesh".

I believe it is healthy to allow yourself time to grieve the death of your dream and the ending of the ideal on which you once built your life and future. There is nothing wrong in doing this and it can help you come to terms with living with your partner in the future.

Bring all the grief in your heart, all the sense of loss, of being let down, of emptiness, of hopelessness and of depression to the foot of the One who hung on the cross to bear the weight of the sin and suffering of the world. Look into his compassionate eyes through your tears of disappointment and hurt and see in him empathy both at your loneliness and at your pain. But look at him longer, for as you look you will begin to see his eyes flicker with hope that he promises is for you, courage to go on in the strength that he holds out to you, and his assurance that he will not let you down. "I will not fail you or forsake you", you can hear him say as you read the Bible and find in it the comfort that he longs to give you.

Immerse yourself in reading through the Psalms at this time. Meet men and women whose experience of life's pain and disappointment mirrors yours, and encounter the God to whom they turned who did not let them down in their distress. Facing reality at this stage and coming to terms with it, can be one of the most important things you ever do for your marriage and for your family.

Remember, there are people around you to whom you can go and talk. It isn't necessary for you to bottle up your grief inside yourself. Possibly within your own church fellowship are others who have faced a similar experience in their marriage, who are willing to give you time to share and pray together. Such support can be crucial. You need to find someone who is discreet and who will keep every word you say in total confidence, for one of the worst things that could happen to you at this stage is for your experience to be gossiped around and perhaps to get back to your partner. Your minister may be the one who can direct you to someone who can help you or himself may be able to encourage you in coming to terms with your grief. Should he find it hard to understand the pain about which you are talking, you could let him read this chapter.

As you come to terms with the loss of your dream, be gentle in what you expect of yourself. Don't set yourself standards which you cannot live up to, as you are still too emotionally fragile to handle the heavy demands you may make on yourself. Give yourself the time you need to accept your life and then step out and begin to live again.

During this coming-to-terms stage, many have found it an immense support and strength to deepen their prayer life and to learn to draw more heavily on God's resources. Soak yourself in the Bible, meditate on parts that seem to be special for you at this time and write them out and carry them around with you so that you can read them wherever you are.

If you are unable to sleep at night, then get up and drink in God's Word and rest in the fact that God is with you – whether you can feel him there or not – and talk to him in prayer as you lie waiting for sleep to come. If sleep is a problem, then don't ask your doctor for sleeping pills for too long. If you are emotionally fragile, go and tell your doctor about it but only ask for tranquillizers as a last resort and for a short time. If you sleep badly for a couple of months, it isn't the end of the world – you won't die and in the end your body will compensate and you will actually sleep far more than you imagine! Plenty of exercise in the evening is as good as anything to help you rest when you face emotional pain.

Tranquillizers will make you feel better, but they won't help the cause of your pain – and it is the cause that really needs treating. Coming to terms with your marriage as it is, and not as you imagined it was going to be, cannot be accomplished effectively if your mind is blurred and its edge blunted by pills that make you feel less miserable than you otherwise would. One of the major problems with tranquillizers is that they are habit-forming, very difficult to stop, and hundreds of Christian women are addicted to them and unable to give them up once they've been on them for a while. So, if your doctor says you need them, check that he won't keep on giving you repeat prescriptions should you demand them, but that he will be tough with you and make sure you don't get hooked!

Chapter 11

Deadlock. Shirley wondered how she could ever have said what she did to Alan. She meant it – every word. But it was something that perhaps she should have kept to herself. Right or wrong, it had now been spoken and she could tell from the silence that hung between the two of them like a dense thorn thicket that Alan had heard and been hurt by every word.

It seemed like the culmination of years and years of being misunderstood, misinterpreted and never really listened to. Of being thought still to be the person that Alan had married twenty-three years ago, and never being seen as the woman she now was who had developed, matured and grown over the years.

The words hung between them: "I want to leave you. I no longer want to continue with our relationship." And Alan said absolutely nothing, leaving Shirley to wonder whether he had heard or whether he hoped that by his silence the words would go away as quickly as they had erupted.

Shirley knew, like so many other wives desperate after twenty or so years of marriage, that while on the one hand she did long for freedom from Alan, it was something that she as a Christian could not really opt for. She knew in her spirit that to leave her husband was to deny something very deep about God's view of marriage. On the one hand her emotional pain cried out for the oblivion of never having to live with him any more, but on the other side her spiritual nature nagged like dull toothache, telling her, "You and he are one flesh in God's eyes. You cannot walk out just because the pathway is so painful. You have no grounds for leaving your husband that would stand biblical scrutiny. To leave Alan would be to deny your heart's desire to follow God closely all your life. And at root, walking out on Alan would be one way of disobeying what you know to be God's command to you."

Shirley is not unique. In common with some other wives whom I know, she has realized that somehow she must find a way in which she can walk through life with Alan. Walk with the pain that being married to Alan will inevitably bring to her, and yet walk not as a martyr but rather as one who finds out of her marriage with pain a life that is positive, joyful, selfless and radiates the God she wholeheartedly follows.

It is one thing to have high ideals and high expectations of marriage. It is another to have to face the reality that ideals and expectations are going to remain unfulfilled – the likelihood of dramatic change for some is very small. To some Christian women this comes as a numbing realization. They and their partner are now so fixed in their ways that it is only in superficial things that they are, humanly speaking, open to change. Deep-seated, lifelong attitudes rarely alter in the late forties, sixties or seventies!

Coming to terms with the fact that change is unlikely can be a struggle, especially for a woman who has worked for years towards building a more deeply loving and caring relationship with her husband. She asks herself, was all the work over all those years a waste? If he has never really heard, never really understood, then why did she go through all the effort of making herself vulnerable by opening herself to help him understand her and hopefully deepen their communication with one another? If he has never heard, never understood, why has she bothered? Wouldn't she have been better employed out at work, decorating the house, gardening, shopping for old people, writing poetry, or running the marathon?

For some women there is the blank emptiness of facing years ahead with a man who does not understand them, and the prospect fills them with a deep desire for annihilation. Life is not worth living very much longer if it has to continue in the company of somebody who can never understand or be understood.

But I believe that it is better for a woman to have tried and failed in this respect than never to have tried at all. I believe that the high view of marriage that some women hold is an important ideal — for it shows that they have grasped the essence of the relationship within the Trinity — as Father, Son and Holy Spirit commune within the Godhead in deep love. And man and woman, created in the image of God, are made to reflect the love that radiates from the heart of the Godhead.

Perhaps because it is part of a woman's nature to be more tuned to the spiritual than most men, a woman is more likely to respond to the picture society around her paints of male and female relationships being something deeper, more communing and more giving than was understood by former generations. Sensing this is part of her spirituality. She perhaps has an awareness that a relationship that has a special quality of depth about it is in some ways a reflection of God's own nature — and she responds intuitively and willingly to concepts about a marriage relationship having a component of deep mutual understanding.

Her husband, however, may be operating along male logical lines. Within him may be implanted a deep-seated desire to succeed at work, to express his masculinity through sport, and to support his family and provide adequately for them. He may never really have felt the need for deep relationships — the very idea may even make him cringe and withdraw into a shell of self-sufficiency. And so, the wife who has been striving to create situations when the two of them can draw closer together, to make atmospheres in which mutual sharing is possible, and to build time into their lifestyle when they can be together, may find after years of trying that her efforts have achieved very little. Such wives are left hurt and confused – trapped with men to whom they cannot relate deeply, bound to them by marriage so that they cannot form deep relationships with others without breaking their marriage vows.

When such a woman reaches the point of knowing that all her trying will never bring about the relationship she needs to make her the full person she believes she has been created to be, and which she believes marriage is intended to provide for her, what does she do? Commit suicide? But is that really the way out of life's intolerable situations?

Many on reaching this point of disillusionment, pain and rejection, respond: "I can't take it any more. I'd rather live alone than go through this kind of living hell." Some leave home for separation and divorce – coupled with the guilt and failure of knowing that they have tried but failed so badly that they have had to give up. Some Christians who have reacted in this way have been left with their faith battered and warped, wondering why God has allowed them to be shackled to such a partner.

Yet others stay with their partner, but find in other people the companionship and love that has been denied them in their marriage. Perhaps they did not originally intend to have an affair at the stage in which they realized their hopelessness. But a man came along who understood and really tried to care – and he stood in such sharp contrast to their partner that overwhelming acceptance, being loved unconditionally, being perceived as beautiful and desirable by another man, caught them unawares and a relationship began that ended in bed.

And yet, God's ideal for men and women is one man, one woman, together for life. What does the woman do who knows this – and for this reason stays with her husband? She may have tried everything she can think of from pulling herself together, making herself as attractive as possible for him, being sexually available in the ways she knows might please him, cooking his favourite meals, serving and waiting on him, but it has made no difference. She may have tried nagging, talking straight, losing her temper and blowing her top. But nothing ever changed. She faces ten, twenty, thirty or forty bleak years of marriage to this man with whom she no longer wants to be. She knows perfectly well that in her late teens or early twenties when she agreed to marry him, she was far too young to make a choice that was to last into her sixties. Yet she is stuck with that choice, made in the immaturity, inexperience and hurriedness of youth.

She may have to face the fact that she has married the wrong man – that on the face of it they are incompatible and, given her time over again, she would never make the same mistake. Their incompatibility may not be in areas that are quantifiable – he may not have abused her sexually, physically or mentally. He may never have been cruel. He may have provided well for her and the children. But now they are two people who, like oil and water, do not mix. Yet, if they stick to their Christian commitment and belief in biblical teaching, they have no reason to leave one another and are doomed to stay together in their incompatibility and unhappiness for another twenty-odd years.

The Christian who has decided that separation is not an option for her is saved the dilemma of the endless "Should I, shouldn't I leave him?" If she has grasped the clear biblical teaching that divorce is permitted only on grounds of adultery and dangerous violence to her or the children, then she faces the prospect of taking the ruins of a marriage and giving it to God for him to take the shattered fragments of her life and out of them to create something worthwhile.

Accepting something that cannot be changed is a major area in which healing can come to a marriage of opposites who have little in common, other perhaps than their belief in the same God. The saying "in acceptance lieth peace" can be the foundation on which healing can begin to flow into the heart of one who is in deep pain. To face the realization that nothing is going to change radically can be a positive and not necessarily a negative stage in the pilgrimage of the woman who can neither live with her husband nor leave him.

Acceptance can bring peace in a far deeper way than the peace that garrisons the heart of a Christian. The word "peace" or *shalom* denotes wholeness and healing. And the simple acceptance that a marriage is as it is, that everything possible has been done to make it different, can in itself be deeply healing. The odd flicker of old hope for things to change for the better cannot be quenched, but its flickering fire need not be fed by wishful daydreaming and endless "if only's".

Acceptance gives many the ability to grit their teeth and say, "Right! If that's so, I'll do my best within these limitations to make the partnership work. It won't be what I've been struggling towards all my life. It won't be what I see marriage should be in terms of reflecting the relationship of the Godhead, or Christ's relationship with the Church, but I will do my best to make it a marriage in which my husband's needs can be met to the best of my ability, and in which he can find peace and some degree of happiness."

The wife who is able to adopt an attitude like this is, I believe, one who really understands the sanctity of marriage and the sacrificial love of Christ that is to be poured out on to the world through his children. She may be able to see little to love in her husband any more – so great has been her pain that he may even be seen as little more than one who causes hurt – and so she shrinks from this and does not want to look at him any more. Yet she can obey the biblical injunction: "Wives submit to your husbands" regardless of whether her husband is obeying the words addressed to him in the same part of Scripture: "Love your wives, just as Christ loved the Church and gave himself up for her . . . love (your) wives as (your) own bodies . . . love (your) wife as (you) love (yourself) . . ."

It is no longer a case of, "If you love me as you should, then I'll do my part . . ." Rather it is, "Regardless of what you do or don't do, I'll respect and submit to you." Such obedience by the Christian to biblical teaching is nowhere qualified by any clauses like, "As long as you get on well together" or, "As long as you feel like it!" The biblical command stands stark and unqualified.

"But, I can't be *commanded* to love someone!" you may respond. "Oh yes you can!" I would reply. I believe that love in the biblical sense has little to do with feelings. Love can be commanded of us because we can be asked to set our wills in a certain direction and to determine that we will act in certain ways. We cannot be commanded to *feel* anything – but we can be commanded to be determined to pursue a loving course of action – namely, to do everything in our power to work for the highest good of another person.

This means that a woman can act lovingly towards the husband for whom she no longer feels anything very much, or towards whom she feels hostile, neutral, or uncaring. And when Jesus commands his followers to "love as I have loved you", such a woman is not exempted in her pathway of discipleship from loving the man whom she feels has ignored and rejected her for many years.

Nowhere does Jesus say: "Love those who are really good to you!" The reverse. He commands: "Love your enemies . . . Do to others as you would have them do to you. If you love those who love you, what credit is that to you? . . . if you do good to those who are good to you, what credit is that to you? . . . Love your enemies, do good to them . . . Be merciful, just as your Father is merciful" (Luke 6:27–36).

For some this will be one of the biggest tests they will ever face as disciples of Jesus. How much easier to walk out on the marriage partner who causes emotional pain and is often perceived more as an enemy than a friend, than to act lovingly towards him. But love is the course of action commanded by the Lord Jesus. And as Lord, his commands are not to be ignored because they appear to be too costly or too difficult for us to try to carry them out. Jesus never promised that Christianity would be a bed of sweet-smelling primroses and violets – rather, he promised the thorns and nails of crucifixion to those who "take up their cross and follow" him. How seriously do some of us take our discipleship? Will we be those who opt out when the price of following our Master seems too steep to pay?

The wife who stays with her husband in this situation is often the woman who lives out in experience Jesus' command to "turn the other cheek". She goes back again, to face the same pain of rejection that she has faced time and time before. She does it in the spirit of humility and love because she wants to please her heavenly Lord who gave his life for her on the cross. In staying with her husband she may begin to see in him and in her service of him, the Lord Jesus himself. The wife who turns her back on her husband may one day herself stand at the judgement seat of Christ and hear him say to her: "I was hungry and you gave me nothing to eat, I was thirsty and you gave me nothing to drink, I was a stranger and you did not invite me in. I needed clothes and you did not clothe me, I was sick and in prison and you did not look after me . . . whatever you did not do for one of the least of these, you did not do for me . . ." (Matthew 25:42–45).

It is tempting to say: "But Lord, he's worse than me . . . look at how he's treated me!" But before the judgement seat of Christ, on the final day, each man and woman stands alone to account for the way in which they have used their individual lives, and to account for their actions to others. At that place there will be no comparison, or passing the blame elsewhere.

The Christian follows the Lord Jesus Christ, who poured out his life in selfless love for men and women who rejected him, despised him, failed to thank him, misunderstood and misinterpreted him, and finally, after an unfair trial, crucified him. This same Jesus says to us: "My command is this: Love each other as I have loved you. Greater love has no one than this, that one lay down his life for his friends" (John 15:12–13).

To live a life of loving action with a partner who has rejected, misunderstood and cared little, is for the Christian a kind of loving that is Jesus' intention. Yet to most of us it seems a highly abnormal way to love. We naturally respond to rejection by retaliation, to constant lovelessness by antipathy, and to misunderstanding by self-pity. But Jesus' way, in the face of all these things, was to go out and actually give his life for those very people who so hurt him. I believe that his followers facing marriage problems can adopt attitudes similar to his.

This realization was a revelation to Shirley in her relationship with Alan. She saw with incredible clarity that it was possible for her to go on living with this man, and that she could obey the biblical command to love him by setting her will to work for his ultimate highest good. Such action did not depend on what she felt but rather on what she intended.

Instead of asking herself any more: "Which of my needs are unmet in Alan?" she began to ask herself what she should not have left unasked for so many years: "What needs has my husband that I haven't noticed or been told about? How can I respond to his needs and learn to meet them regardless of whether he does or doesn't understand me or meet my own needs?" Instead of reacting as in the past – "he didn't even notice how I was feeling – " and sinking into depressed silence or nagging criticism, she began to try to ignore her own need for understanding love and to try to learn to pour out her love on him regardless of what she felt.

"Nothing changed overnight!" she told me. "It was hard sweat, blood and tears. My old habits and thought patterns didn't change because I had decided to be different to Alan. But the Holy Spirit has started something in me, and I want to be open to allowing him to change me radically."

For her, this major step in reorientating her thinking was marked by a small, yet significant symbolic step. "For years I knitted myself sweaters. The fact that I didn't knit for him somehow was a silent statement – to myself as no one else noticed – that I never knitted for him because we weren't the 'one flesh' I longed for us to be. The day that I went out and chose knitting wool and a pattern and started to knit a sweater that I hoped would please him, marked the day on which I deliberately chose to put him first and deliberately began to try to forget myself as much as I could."

Shirley had discovered the secret of working out a marriage that is not what you expect it to be – a simple but profound secret. Simply, that if you want your marriage to change then you have to change yourself – not your partner! And with that change, for the majority, comes learning to die to self and learning to live at home the selfless love that reflects the life of Jesus Christ.

"I don't want to do that for him . . . he can do it himself . . ." comes as the challenge to any following such a pathway. In a whispered voice, heard only in the heart, come Jesus' words in reply: "I washed my disciples' feet . . . surely you can serve him in just that small way."

For the Christian learning to live in such a way with a marriage partner, this can be a profoundly spiritual experience. It involves an identification with Jesus Christ in his death on the cross, by the daily deaths of dying to self and living for another. And the Christian discovers very soon, as his feet traverse this pathway, that he cannot attain any of this on his own. It seems the more he tries, the more he fails! The more Shirley tried to serve Alan the harder it got – the less he appeared to notice and appreciate her and the more she longed to hurl a saucepan at his head and scream: "Haven't you noticed what I'm trying to be? Can't you see the difference?"

Alan, according to her, was even more lost in his own world and even less observant of her than ever before. "It got to the point where I could only weep silently in prayer: 'Dear God, please fill me with your Holy Spirit and live your life out through me, because I can't do this on my own.'"

Shirley began to find that as she had asked God to change her, so he began to show her unpleasant areas in her personality that needed altering. Her prayer: "Lord change me . . ." had been heard by God and was taken so seriously that she began to glimpse the kind of person she needed to be transformed into if Alan was to have the kind of wife that God intended.

"What about your own unmet needs?" I asked her.

Her brown eyes clouded for a second, meeting mine and then looking away quickly. "They remain unmet . . . but I'm surviving . . . and I do believe that God is able to take care of my needs. It's not for me to fight for my rights as a wife to have certain things from my husband . . . it's up to me to love him and to leave God to deal with those needs of mine that go unmet as long as I am Alan's wife – which will be till death do us part."

In a world screaming for women's rights to be taken seriously and given totally, Shirley's words sound strange. Yet, it was a male Christian who first spoke of the Christian's choice either to cling on to his rights or to freely give them up. "Don't we have the right to food and drink? Don't we have the right to take a believing wife along with us . . ? If others have this right of support from you, shouldn't we have it all the more? But we did not use this right. On the contrary, we put up with anything rather than hinder the Gospel of Christ . . . but I have not used any of these rights . . ." said the Apostle Paul (1 Corinthians 9:4,5,12,15).

Christian husbands and wives do have certain rights that are to be expected in marriage. Sexual intercourse is one such right that is encouraged and only to be stopped for a brief time by mutual consent "so that you may devote yourself to prayer" (1 Corinthians 7:5). Christians have rights in the same way as anyone else, and our society has taught us that in marriage today's partners have the right to expect fulfilment, understanding and companionship in each other.

When Shirley decided to try to allow God to change her whole attitude towards her marriage, and to try to make it work in a different, revolutionary way, she deliberately chose to give up many of those rights which she had assumed automatically to be hers. "Have we no rights?" she asked herself. "Yes – we have rights. But I choose to give up many of my rights, for Jesus' sake, so that I can be more truly loving in a self-giving way to Alan."

"What about him?" I wanted to know.

"I have to leave that to God. I'm asking God to change me, not to change Alan!" She smiled.

When I played devil's advocate with the words, "It sounds all right in theory but what are you doing in practice?" she began to reel off a list of things like, "I'll give him a fiftieth birthday party – and not expect him to do the same for me; I'll take on some of the things he does around the house and hates doing, and I'll try not to let him notice; when he forgets to do things, I'll do them for him and not even tell him he's forgotten; I'll make sure that by the time he gets to do some things they are done already and he probably won't even notice I've done them. But that isn't the point, is it? It is loving him and serving him . . . not looking for his appreciation – that's the way in which I want to try and make things work from now onwards."

"What you're looking for is a miracle in you, isn't it?" I wanted to know.

"It has to be that", she agreed. "I can't possibly stick out at a marriage like this, let alone do all these things to change unless God miraculously transforms me . . . and I'm depending on him to do just that. After all, he has said that when we are helpless we are the most strong, because in our helplessness God is able to pour his transforming grace and strength into us . . . and that's my only hope!" (see 2 Corinthians 12:10).

Talking to Shirley, I had a deep sense that she had got what it takes! She had seen her marriage and how to make it work from what, to a human point of view, was a ludicrous perspective – but with God's grace and in God's economy it was a perspective that just could work and could save her and Alan from being yet another one of the one-in-three divorce statistic.

I pray so!

Epilogue

The seven-year-old nestled closer to his great-grandfather, for the wind howling down Mile End Road was as bitter as it had been when I was a child about a century earlier. I understood with the certainty that comes only in a dream that I was seeing the future, and no one therefore had to tell me that the fair-haired youngster was my own great-great-grandson. Nor did it seem in the least unusual to be watching the oddly assorted pair as they progressed down the road.

They did not need to tell me that they were drawn irresistibly back to the source of our roots – the East End of London.

The old man was pointing to a grey building, "That's where your great-grandpa was a student", he explained to the lad.

Moving along the road he turned down a side street, "Down there is the library where your great-great-great-grandpa was chief librarian . . . that was before they put all the books on to computer and when you still had to read them on paper . . ."

The old man then stopped for a long time looking at the front of a building, now converted into flats but bearing on its frontage the old design showing what it once had been. "That was a music hall", he slowly explained.

The boy's face was blank. "What's that?" he asked.

"When my mother was young," the old man replied, "they had these places where you could go and watch dancing and singing on a stage . . . but my mum told me that her great-grandfather hired that hall every Sunday night to use it as a rescue mission for down-and-outs . . . he used to talk to them about Jesus . . ."

"The same Jesus that you and gran tell me about?" the boy asked. The old man nodded.

"But where are all these people of mine now?" the boy questioned.

"In heaven with Jesus", said the old man firmly.

"Where's their bodies?" the boy wanted to know.

"In the graveyard", replied my son. "Come on . . . it's only a few miles from here and I'll show you something special . . . the place where lots of your relatives were buried in the old days . . ."

My dream followed the couple as they turned off the cement road, through the concrete jungles of high-rise flats and into the grassy place from an era long past, where the dead were buried before they were all cremated as in the time about which when I was dreaming.

"Here it is", the old man's face lit up. "This is our family place just here. You read the words out aloud as my eyes aren't good enough for the old worn lettering . . ."

The lad slowly read the messages on the gravestones, and the old man closed his eyes remembering his loved ones who no longer lived on this earth.

"But grandpa," the lad's questions began again, "why does it say so many times 'beloved wife of . . .' or 'much loved husband of . . .'? What about all their other husbands and wives?"

The old man's face clouded, and he put his gnarled hands around the boy's shoulders. "Son," he said, "in those days it was very, very good. Your relatives only had one husband or wife . . ."

"How do you mean?" the boy was anxious to know.

"When someone married they stayed with that person for life. That meant that each child just had one mum and dad and lived with them until they grew up, married and left home."

"No step mothers and fathers?" asked the boy, his eyes wistful.

"That's right . . . just one mum and dad all your life", replied the old man. "God really made it to be like that, and that's how it was for most people in the old days . . ."

The boy ran his supple fingers over the weather-worn lettering on the family graves, as if he was savouring the moment and would cherish the memory of his relatives who had been together as complete families for most of their lives. "Wish it was like that today . . . I don't like my new mummy . . ." he commented.

"When you get married you can change it", the old man said slowly. "You can change it back into how it was meant to be when God gave woman to man in marriage. You don't have to leave things as they are . . ."

Then suddenly the penetrating bleep, bleep of my electronic alarm shut off the dream and returned me to the land of the present.

"I had a funny dream", I tried to tell my husband. "It was about our future relatives and what marriage could be like for them . . ." I explained as best I could.

"Never mind," said my ever practical husband, "we don't have to let marriage deteriorate to that extent. If we get it right ourselves then our descendants will have a pattern to copy . . ."

And, as usual, I realized he was right! The future of marriage was in our hands and in the hands of others like us. If we made it work out, then we would be giving our children and our children's children a precious gift . . . but it was up to us.

The future of marriage was by no means irrevocably set to deteriorate or to improve by any law of the universe. God had shown us his plan – it was up to us to follow his design or to go our own ways. But the choice we made was a serious one for it affected more than us alone – we were making choices that would deeply affect future generations.

"We've got to get it right!" I stated with determination.

"With God's help we'll try our best", he replied. "And if enough of us do, we'll give our descendants a legacy worth having . . ."

References

Chapter 2
1. Robert Runcie writing in: *Church of England Newspaper*, 6 July 1984
2. "Values and the Changing Family" (Study Commission on the Family), p.42

Chapter 3
1. Jack Dominian, *Make Or Break* (SPCK, 1984), p.25
2. *Ibid.*, pp.28–9
3. Paul Tournier, *Marriage Difficulties* (Highland Books, 1984), p.29
4. *Ibid.*, pp.21–2

Chapter 4
1. Helmut Thielicke, *The Ethics of Sex* (James Clarke, 1978), pp. 307–8
2. William Barclay, *The Plain Man's Guide to Ethics* (Fount Paperbacks, 1973), pp.119ff
3. John Stott, *Issues Facing Christians Today* (Marshall, 1984), p.241
4. Martin Luther, *The Sermon on the Mount*, Luther's Works, Vol. 21 (Concordia, 1956), p.23
5. James B. Hurley, *Man and Woman in Biblical Perspective* (IVP, 1981), p.77
6. Elizabeth Catherwood writing in: Shirley Lees (ed.), *The Role of Women* (IVP, 1984), pp.26–7
7. John Stott, *op. cit.*, p.245
8. James Hurley, *op. cit.*, pp.206–14
9. *Ibid.*, p.151
10. Richard Winter, *The Roots of Sorrow* (Marshall, 1984), p.278

Chapter 5
1. Marsha Rowe (ed.), *A Spare Rib Reader* (Penguin, 1982), p.574

2. "Social Trends 1985" (HMSO), p.60
3. Cary Cooper and Marilyn Davidson, *High Pressure, The Working Lives of Women Managers* (Fontana, 1982), p.199
4. Josey Bass, *Three Hundred Eminent Personalities* (San Francisco, 1978)
5. Gail Sheehy, *Pathfinders* (Bantam Books, 1981), p.153
6. Anne Dickenson, *A Woman in Your Own Right* (Quartet Books, 1982), p.xi
7. Alvin Toffler, *The Third Wave* (Collins, 1980), p.239
8. *Ibid.*, p.241
9. Ann Dally, *Inventing Motherhood* (Burnett Books, 1982), pp.18,20
10. Ferdinand Mount, *The Subversive Family* (Jonathan Cape, 1982), p.255

Chapter 6

1. John Stott, *Issues Facing Christians Today*, *op. cit.*, p.248
2. *Ibid.*, p.248
3. *Ibid.*, p.247
4. *The Role of Women*, *op. cit.*, p.36
5. *Ibid.*, pp.70–1
6. *Ibid.*, p.44
7. Larry and Nordis Christenson, *The Christian Couple* (Kingsway, 1978), p.160
8. *The Role of Women*, *op. cit.*, p.61

Chapter 7

1. A.C. Thiselton writing in: Colin Brown (ed.), *Dictionary of New Testament Theology*, Vol. 1 (Paternoster, 1975), p.678
2. *Ibid.*, p.672
3. Gerhard von Rad, *Genesis* (SCM, 1978), p.85
4. Derek Kidner, *Genesis* (IVP, 1976), pp.66,69
5. John Burnaby, *Christian Words and Christian Meanings* (Hodder & Stoughton, 1966), p.52
6. Helmut Thielicke, *The Ethics of Sex*, *op. cit.*, pp.81ff
7. Paul Tournier, *Marriage Difficulties*, *op. cit.*, p.29
8. *Ibid.*, p.33
9. *Ibid.*, p.36
10. Jack Dominian, *Make or Break*, *op. cit.*, p.36
11. Paul Tournier, *op. cit.*, p.53
12. *Ibid.*, p.58
13. *Ibid.*, p.64

Chapter 8
1. Morgan Derham writing in: *Daily Notes* (Scripture Union, 1985), pp.48ff
2. Helmut Thielicke, *The Ethics of Sex, op. cit.*, p.95
3. Paul Tournier, *Marriage Difficulties, op. cit.*, p.45
4. *Ibid.*, p.46
5. *Ibid.*, p.46
6. Morgan Derham, *op. cit.*, p.54

Chapter 9
1. John Powell, *Why Am I Afraid to Love?*, Fount, 1975
2. First published in *Family* magazine, 1984
3. First published in *Family* magazine, 1984

Chapter 10
1. These thoughts first published in *Family* magazine, 1984
2. Jack Dominian, *Make or Break, op. cit.*, p.57

Also available in Fount Paperbacks

The Mind of St Paul
WILLIAM BARCLAY

'There is a deceptive simplicity about this fine exposition of Pauline thought at once popular and deeply theological. The Hebrew and Greek backgrounds are described and all the main themes are lightly but fully treated.'   *The Yorkshire Post*

The Plain Man Looks at the Beatitudes
WILLIAM BARCLAY

'. . . the author's easy style should render it . . . valuable and acceptable to the ordinary reader.'   *Church Times*

The Plain Man Looks at the Lord's Prayer
WILLIAM BARCLAY

Professor Barclay shows how this prayer that Jesus gave to his disciples is at once a summary of Christian teaching and a pattern for all prayers.

The Plain Man's Guide to Ethics
WILLIAM BARCLAY

The author demonstrates beyond all possible doubt that the Ten Commandments are the most relevant document in the world today and are totally related to mankind's capacity to live and make sense of it all within a Christian context.

Ethics in a Permissive Society
WILLIAM BARCLAY

How do we as Christians deal with such problems as drug taking, the 'pill', alcohol, morality of all kinds, in a society whose members are often ignorant of the Church's teaching? Professor Barclay approaches a difficult and vexed question with his usual humanity and clarity, asking what Christ himself would say or do in our world today.

Also available in Fount Paperbacks

BOOKS BY RITA SNOWDEN

Discoveries That Delight

'Thirty brief chapters of reflections on selected psalms . . . The
book is very readable. Its style has been achieved through many
years of work to produce a vehicle of religious communication
with a wide appeal.'

Neville Ward, Church of England Newspaper

Further Good News

'Another enjoyable book from Rita Snowden; easy to read and
with a store of good things to ponder over and store in the mind.
The author shows clearly that there is much Good News in our
world and that this is very much the gift of a loving God.'

Church Army Review

I Believe Here and Now

'Once again she has produced for us one of the most readable and
helpful pieces of Christian witness I have seen . . .'

D. P. Munro, Life and Work

A Woman's Book of Prayer

'This book will make prayer more real and meaningful for all who
use it. There is all through the book an accent of reality. Here the
needs of the twentieth century are brought to God in twentieth
century language.'

William Barclay

More Prayers for Women

'. . . she has that rare and valuable gift of being able to compose
forms of prayer which really do express the aspirations of many
people . . .'

Philip Cecil, Church Times

Also available in Fount Paperbacks

Fount Paperbacks

Fount is one of the leading paperback publishers of religious books and below are some of its recent titles.

- [ ] THE WAY OF ST FRANCIS Murray Bodo £2.50
- [ ] GATEWAY TO HOPE Maria Boulding £1.95
- [ ] LET PEACE DISTURB YOU Michael Buckley £1.95
- [ ] DEAR GOD, MOST OF THE TIME YOU'RE QUITE NICE Maggie Durran £1.95
- [ ] CHRISTIAN ENGLAND VOL 3 David L Edwards £4.95
- [ ] A DAZZLING DARKNESS Patrick Grant £3.95
- [ ] PRAYER AND THE PURSUIT OF HAPPINESS Richard Harries £1.95
- [ ] THE WAY OF THE CROSS Richard Holloway £1.95
- [ ] THE WOUNDED STAG William Johnston £2.50
- [ ] YES, LORD I BELIEVE Edmund Jones £1.75
- [ ] THE WORDS OF MARTIN LUTHER KING Coretta Scott King (Ed) £1.75
- [ ] BOXEN C S Lewis £4.95
- [ ] THE CASE AGAINST GOD Gerald Priestland £2.75
- [ ] A MARTYR FOR THE TRUTH Grazyna Sikorska £1.95
- [ ] PRAYERS IN LARGE PRINT Rita Snowden £2.50
- [ ] AN IMPOSSIBLE GOD Frank Topping £1.95
- [ ] WATER INTO WINE Stephen Verney £2.50

All Fount paperbacks are available at your bookshop or newsagent, or they can be ordered by post from Fount Paperbacks, Cash Sales Department, G.P.O. Box 29, Douglas, Isle of Man, British Isles. Please send purchase price, plus 15p per book, maximum postage £3. Customers outside the U.K. send purchase price, plus 15p per book. Cheque, postal or money order. No currency.

NAME (Block letters) _____

ADDRESS _____

_____